# THE EASY SIXTIES FAKE BOOK

## Melody, Lyrics and Simplified Chords

100 Songs in  '60s the Key of "C"

# THE EASY SIXTIES FAKE BOOK

ISBN 978-0-634-09029-5

HAL•LEONARD®
CORPORATION
7777 W. BLUEMOUND RD. P.O. BOX 13819 MILWAUKEE, WI 53213

Visit Hal Leonard Online at
**www.halleonard.com**

# THE EASY SIXTIES FAKE BOOK

## CONTENTS

# INTRODUCTION

## What Is a Fake Book?

A fake book has one-line music notation consisting of melody, lyrics and chord symbols. This lead sheet format is a "musical shorthand" which is an invaluable resource for all musicians—hobbyists to professionals.

Here's how *The Easy Sixties Fake Book* differs from most standard fake books:

- All songs are in the key of C.

- Many of the melodies have been simplified.

- Only five basic chord types are used—major, minor, seventh, diminished and augmented.

- The music notation is larger for ease of reading.

In the event that you haven't used chord symbols to create accompaniment, or your experience is limited, a chord speller chart is included at the back of the book to help you get started.

Have fun!

# ABRAHAM, MARTIN AND JOHN

Words and Music by
RICHARD HOLLER

# ALONG COMES MARY

Words and Music by
TANDYN ALMER

# B-A-B-Y

Words and Music by DAVID PORTER
and ISAAC HAYES

**Moderate Rock**

1. Ba - by, oh ba - by, _____ I
2., 3. *(See additional lyrics)*

love to call __ you ba - by. __ Ba - by, oh __ ba -

- by, _____ I love _____ for you to call __ me ba -

- by. _____ When you squeeze me real __ tight, _____ you make __

_____ the wrong things __ right. _____ And I can't stop

lov - ing you, _____ and I won't stop want - ing you. 2. Ba -

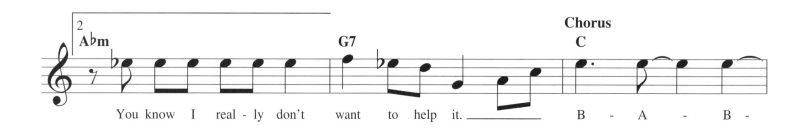

You know I real-ly don't want to help it. _____ B - A - B -

- Y, ba - by, B - A - B - Y, ba - by.

When-ev - er the sun ____ don't shine ____ you throw out the

life - line. ____ Then I get real close to you, ____ and

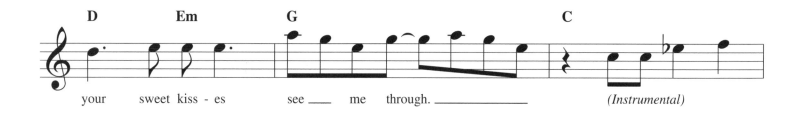

your sweet kiss - es see __ me through. ____ (Instrumental)

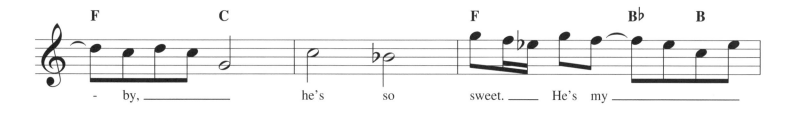

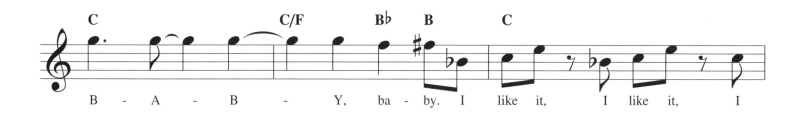

*Additional Lyrics*

2. Baby, oh baby, you look so good to me, baby.
   Baby, oh baby, you are so good to me, baby.
   Just one look in your eyes and my temperature goes sky high.
   I weep for you and can't help it.
   You know I really don't want to help it.
   *To Chorus*

3. I said, baby, oh baby, you look so good to me, baby.
   Baby, oh baby, how I love for you to call me baby.
   When you squeeze me real tight you know you make the wrong things right.
   And I can't stop loving you,
   And I won't stop wanting you.
   *To Coda*

# BABY LOVE

Words and Music by BRIAN HOLLAND,
EDWARD HOLLAND and LAMONT DOZIER

miss - ing ya, miss _____ kiss - ing ya. In - stead of
warm _____ em - brace my love. Don't throw our

break - ing up, _____ let's start some kiss - ing and
love a - way, _____ please don't do

mak - ing up. _____ Don't throw our love a - way. _____
me this way. _____ Not hap - py like I used to be. _____

In my arms why don't you stay?
Lone - li - ness has got the best of

**CODA**

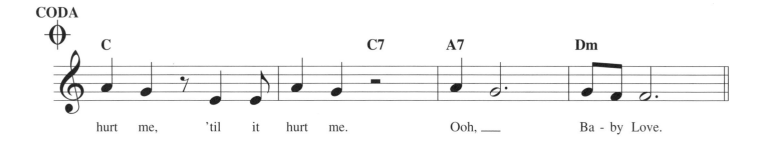

hurt me, 'til it hurt me. Ooh, ___ Ba - by Love.

Don't throw our love a - way.

# BABY, IT'S YOU

Words and Music by MACK DAVID,
BURT BACHARACH and BARNEY WILLIAMS

**Moderately slow**

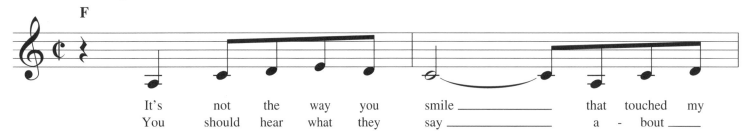

It's not the way you smile _____ that touched my
You should hear what they say _____ a - bout _____

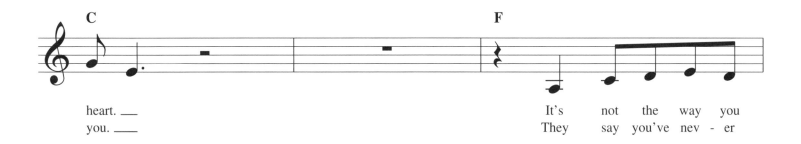

heart. ____
you. ____

It's not the way you
They say you've nev - er

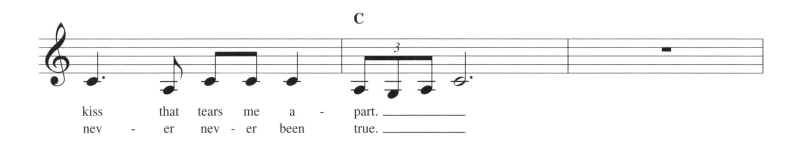

kiss that tears me a - part. _____
nev - er nev - er been true. _____

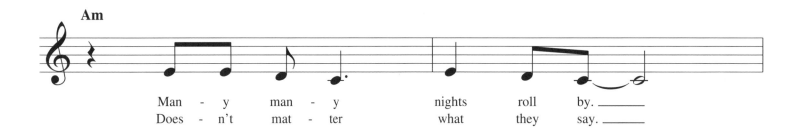

Man - y man - y nights roll by. _____
Does - n't mat - ter what they say. _____

I sit a - lone _____ at home and cry _____ o - ver
I know I'm gon - na love you an - y old way, _____ what can I

you.  What can I do? ___  I can't help my -

self, ___  'cause, ba - by, it's you, ___

ba - by, it's you. ___

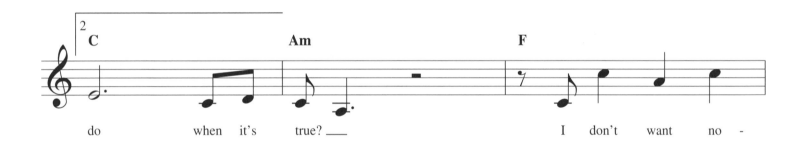

do when it's true? ___  I don't want no -

bod - y,  'cause, ba - by, it's you, ___

ba - by, it's you. ___

# BARBARA ANN

Words and Music by
FRED FASSERT

**Bright Rock tempo**

(Bar - bar Ann, Bar - bar - bar Ann, Bar - bar Ann, Bar - bar - bar Ann.) Bar - bar

Ann, _____ take ___ my hand. _____ Bar - bar

Ann, _____ you got me rock-in' and a-roll-in', rock - in' and a-roll-in', Bar-bar

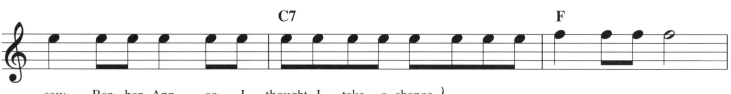

Ann, Bar - bar - bar - bar - bar Ann.
{ Went to a dance, look - in' for ro-mance,
{ Played my fav-'rite tune, danced with Bet - ty Lu,

saw Bar - bar Ann, so I thought I take a chance, } Oh, Bar - bar Ann, Bar - bar Ann,
tried Peg - gy Sue, but I knew they would-n't do. }

take my hand. Oh, Bar - bar Ann, Bar - bar Ann, take my hand. You got me

**2nd time**
**D.C. al Fine**

rock-in' and a-roll-in', rock - in' and a-roll-in', Bar-bar Ann, Bar - bar - bar - bar - bar Ann.

# CYCLES

Words and Music by
GAYLE CALDWELL

# (It's A)
# BEAUTIFUL MORNING

Words and Music by FELIX CAVALIERE
and EDWARD BRIGATI, JR.

**Moderately**

It's a beau - ti - ful morn - ing. _____ Ah!
morn - ing. _____ Ah!

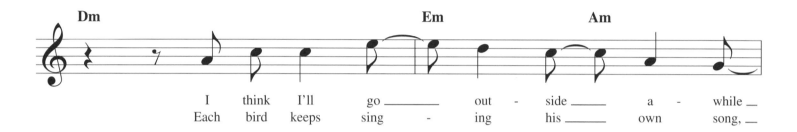

I think I'll go _____ out - side _____ a - while _
Each bird keeps sing - ing his _____ own song, _

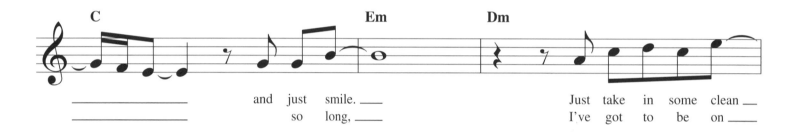

_____ and just smile. ___ Just take in some clean _
_____ so long, ___ I've got to be on _____

_____ fresh air _____ 'cause no sense in stay - ing in - side ___ if the
_____ my way _ now. No good just hang - ing a - round, _ I've got to

weath - er's fine and you've got the time. _____ It's your chance to
cov - er ground you could - n't keep me down. _____ It just ain't no

wake up and plan _ an - oth - er brand - new day. (Ei - ther way.) It's a beau - ti - ful
good if the sun _ shines and you're

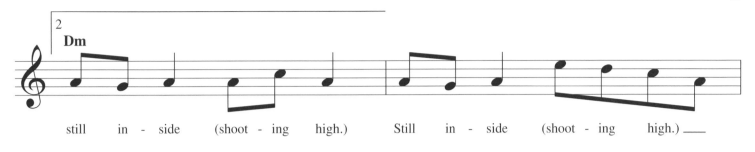

still in - side (shoot - ing high.) Still in - side (shoot - ing high.) ___

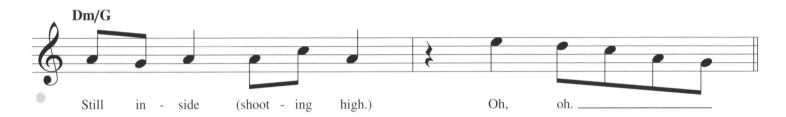

Still in - side (shoot - ing high.) Oh, oh. ___

Ah. ___

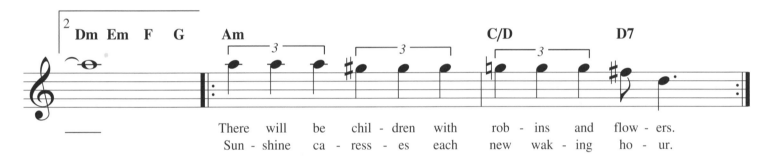

___ There will be chil - dren with rob - ins and flow - ers.
Sun - shine ca - ress - es each new wak - ing ho - ur.

Seems to me ___ that peo - ple keep see - ing more and more to - day. (Got - ta say.)

Lead the way. (It's o - kay.) ___ Got - ta say (Got - ta say.) It's o - kay. (All the way.)

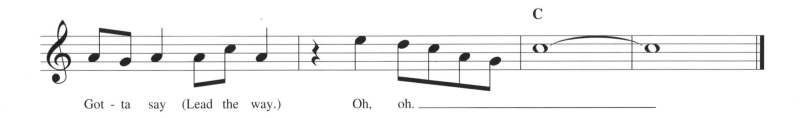

Got - ta say (Lead the way.) Oh, oh. ___

# BEYOND THE SEA

Words and Music by CHARLES TRENET,
ALBERT LASRY and JACK LAWRENCE

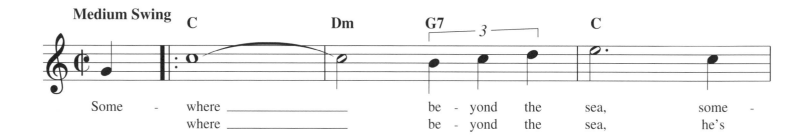

Some - where _____ be - yond the sea, some -
where _____ be - yond the sea, he's

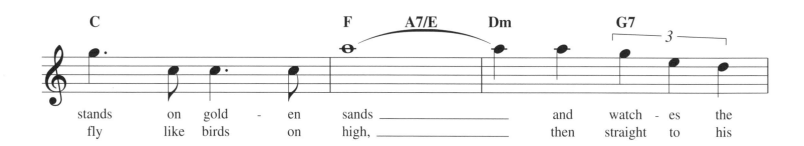

where wait - ing for me, _____ my lov - er
there watch - ing for me. _____ If I could

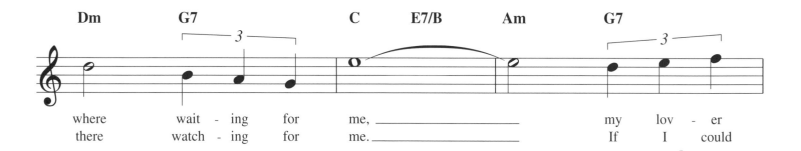

stands on gold - en sands _____ and watch - es the
fly like birds on high, _____ then straight to his

ships that go sail - ing, Some -
arms I'd go sail -

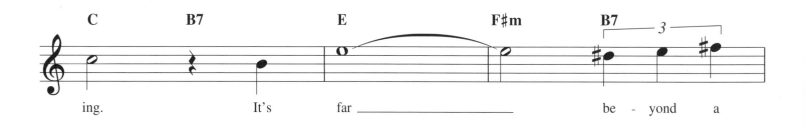

ing. It's far _____ be - yond a

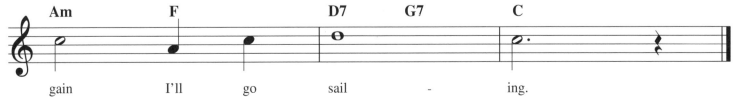

# BLUE VELVET

Words and Music by BERNIE WAYNE
and LEE MORRIS

**Slowly, with tender expression**

She wore blue vel - vet, blu - er than vel - vet was the

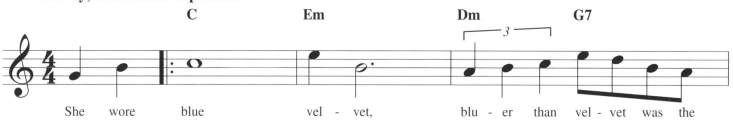

night.   Soft - er than sat - in was the light from the

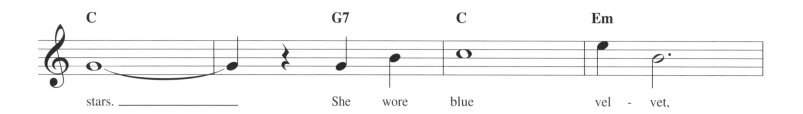

stars. _____ She wore blue vel - vet,

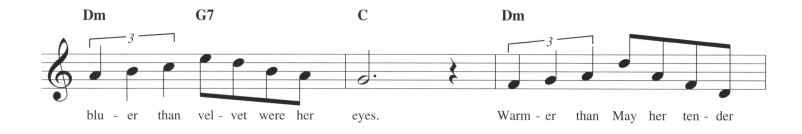

blu - er than vel - vet were her eyes.   Warm - er than May her ten - der

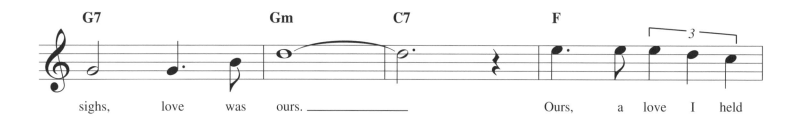

sighs, love was ours. _____ Ours, a love I held

tight - ly, feel - ing the rap - ture grow

like    a    flame    burn - ing    bright - ly.    But    when    she    left,

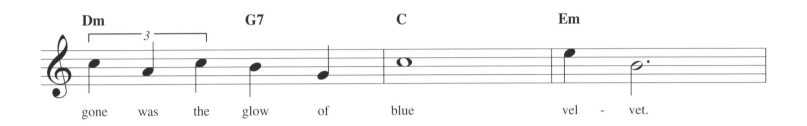

gone    was    the    glow    of    blue    vel - vet.

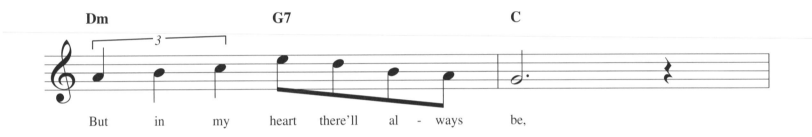

But    in    my    heart    there'll    al - ways    be,

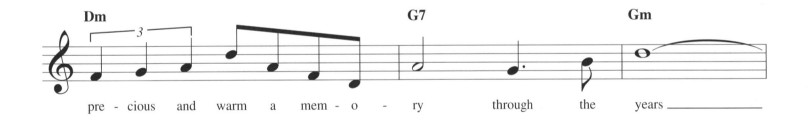

pre - cious    and    warm    a    mem - o - ry    through    the    years _____

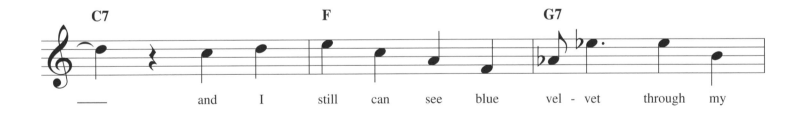

_____    and    I    still    can    see    blue    vel - vet    through    my

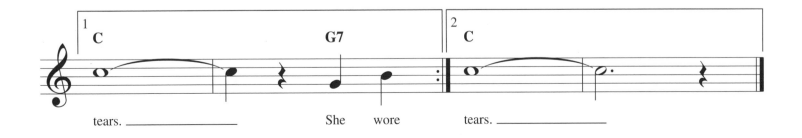

tears. _____    She    wore    tears. _____

# BORN TO BE WILD
## from EASY RIDER

Words and Music by
MARS BONFIRE

**Moderate Rock beat**

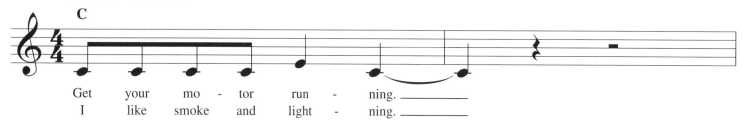

Get your mo - tor run - ning. ____
I like smoke and light - ning. ____

Head out on the high - way ____ look - ing for ad - ven - ture
Heav - y met - al thun - der ____ rac - ing in the wind

in what - ev - er comes our way. ____
and the feel - ing that I'm un - der. ____

Yeah, dar - ling, gon - na make it hap - pen,

take the world in a love em - brace. _ Fire _ all of your guns _

# BROWN EYED GIRL

Words and Music by
VAN MORRISON

**Moderately**

1. Hey, where did we _____ go?         Days _____ when the rains _____
2., 3. *(See additional lyrics)*

_____ came,                down _____ in the hol - low

play - in' a new _____ game,                laugh - ing and a -

run - ning, hey, _____ hey,                skip - ping and a - jump - ing.

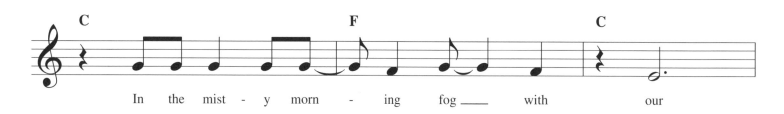

In the mist - y morn - ing fog _____ with                our

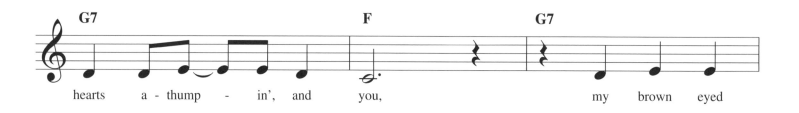

hearts a - thump - in', and you,                my brown eyed

girl. _____                You, my                brown eyed girl. _____

Do you re - mem - ber when

**Chorus**

we used to sing: ___ sha la ___ la la ___ la la ___ la la ___

___ la la la te da. ___ Sha la ___ la la ___

___ la la ___ la la ___ la la la te da ___ la te da. ___

*Additional Lyrics*

2. Whatever happened to Tuesday and so slow
   Going down the old mine with a transistor radio
   Standing in the sunlight laughing
   Hiding behind a rainbow's wall
   Slipping and a-sliding
   All along the waterfall
   With you, my brown eyed girl
   You, my brown eyed girl.
   Do you remember when we used to sing:
   *Chorus*

3. So hard to find my way, now that I'm all on my own
   I saw you just the other day, my, how you have grown
   Cast my memory back there, Lord
   Sometime I'm overcome thinking 'bout
   Making love in the green grass
   Behind the stadium
   With you, my brown eyed girl
   With you, my brown eyed girl.
   Do you remember when we used to sing:
   *Chorus*

# BY THE TIME I GET TO PHOENIX

Words and Music by
JIMMY WEBB

By the time _____ I get to Phoe - nix she'll be
time I make Al - bu - quer - que she'll be
time I make Ok - la - ho - ma she'll be

ri - sin', _____ she'll ___ find the note I left
work - in', _____ she'll ___ pro - 'bly stop at
sleep - in', _____ she'll turn soft - ly and

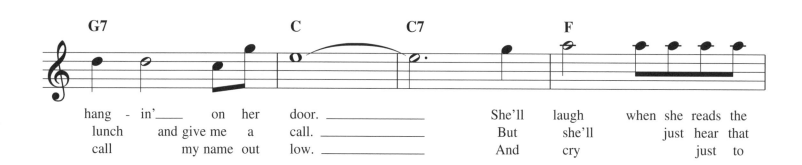

hang - in' ____ on her door. _____ She'll laugh when she reads the
lunch and give me a call. _____ But she'll just hear that
call my name out low. _____ And cry just to

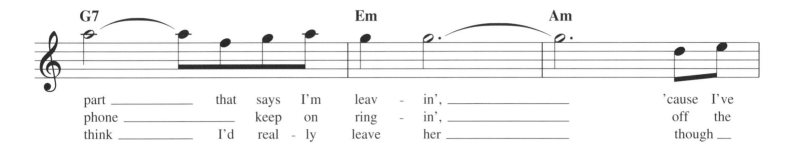

part _____ that says I'm leav - in', _____ 'cause I've

phone _____ keep on ring - in', _____ off the

think _____ I'd real - ly leave her _____ though __

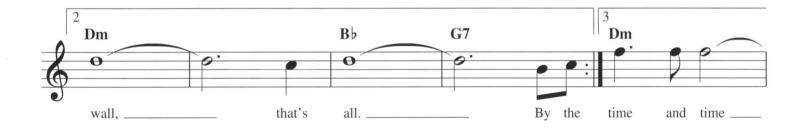

left that girl so man - y times be - fore. _____ By the

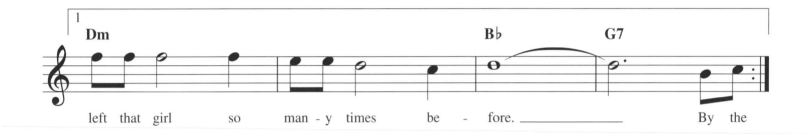

wall, _____ that's all. _____ By the time and time __

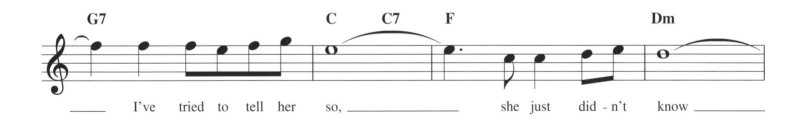

_____ I've tried to tell her so, _____ she just did - n't know _____

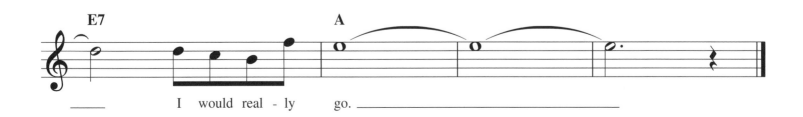

_____ I would real - ly go. _____

# CALIFORNIA GIRLS

Words and Music by BRIAN WILSON
and MIKE LOVE

**Moderate Shuffle Rock**

Well, east coast girls are hip; I real-ly dig those styles they
west coast has the sun-shine and the girls all get so

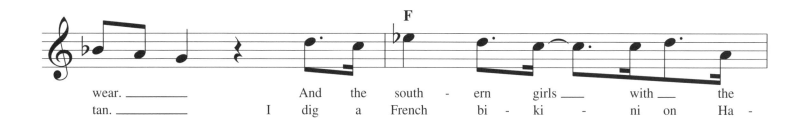

wear. _____ And the south-ern girls _____ with _____ the
tan. _____ I dig a French bi-ki-ni on Ha-

way they talk, _____ they knock me out when I'm down there. _____ The
wai-ian is-lands, dolls by a palm tree in the sand. _____ I

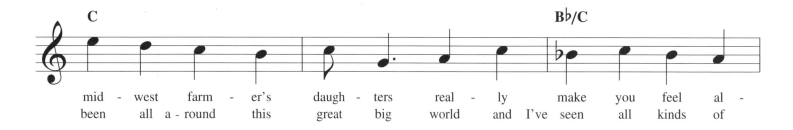

mid-west farm-er's daugh-ters real-ly make you feel al-
been all a-round this great big world and I've seen all kinds of

right, _____ and _____ north-ern girls _____ with _____ the
girls, _____ but I could-n't wait _____ to _____ get

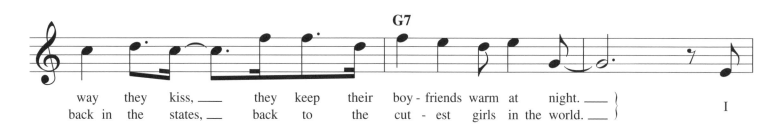

way they kiss, _____ they keep their boy-friends warm at night. _____ }
back in the states, _____ back to the cut-est girls in the world. _____ }

I

# CALL ME

Words and Music by
TONY HATCH

**Moderately**

If you're feel - ing sad and lone - ly,
When it seems your friends de - sert _____ you,
If you call, I'll be right with _____ you.

there's a serv - ice I _____ can ren - der.
there's some - bod - y think - ing of _____ you.
You and I should be _____ to - geth - er.

Tell the one who loves _____ you on - ly
I'm the one who'll nev - er hurt _____ you.
Take this love I long _____ to give _____ you,

I can be so warm _____ and ten - der.
May - be that's be - cause _____ I love you.
I'll be at your side _____ for - ev - er.

Call me! _____ Don't be a - fraid; _____ you can call me. _____

**Fm** ........ **A♭** ........ **To Coda ⊕** **Fm**

May - be it's late, ___ but just call me. ___ Tell me and I'll ___ be a -

**1** **C** ........ **2** **C**

round. _____ round. _____ Now don't for -

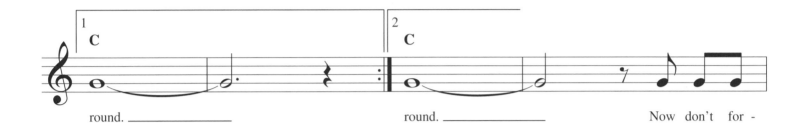

**Dm** **G7** **Dm** **G7** **C**

get me, ___ 'cause if you let me, ___ I will al - ways stay by

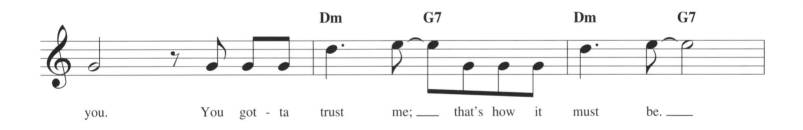

**Dm** **G7** **Dm** **G7**

you. You got - ta trust me; ___ that's how it must be. ___

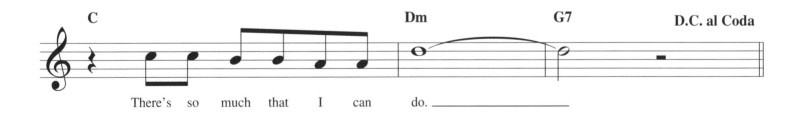

**C** **Dm** **G7** **D.C. al Coda**

There's so much that I can do. _____

**CODA**

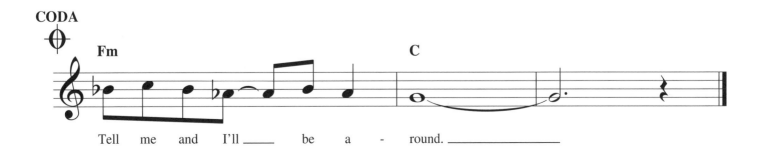

**Fm** **C**

Tell me and I'll ___ be a - round. _____

# CAN'T TAKE MY EYES OFF OF YOU

Words and Music by BOB CREWE
and BOB GAUDIO

# CARRIE-ANNE

Words and Music by ALLAN CLARKE,
TONY HICKS and GRAHAM NASH

# DANCING IN THE STREET

Words and Music by MARVIN GAYE,
IVY HUNTER and WILLIAM STEVENSON

**Steady Rock**

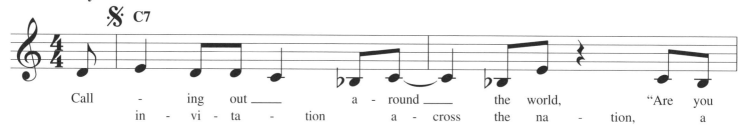

Call - ing out _____ a - round _____ the world, "Are you
in - vi - ta - tion a - cross the na - tion, a

read - y for a brand - new beat?" _____ Sum - mer's here, _____ and the
chance _____ for the folks to meet. _____ There'll be laugh - ing, _____ sing - ing, and

time is right _____ for danc - ing _____ in the streets. _____
mu - sic swing - ing and danc - ing _____ in the streets. _____

_____ They're danc - ing in _____ Chi - ca - go, _____ down in
_____ Phil - a - del - phia P. A., _____ Bal - ti - more and D. C., _____

New Or - leans, _____ up in New York Cit - y. All _____
_____ now, _____ and if we get to Mo - tor Cit - y. All _____

we need ____ is mu - sic, sweet mu - sic. ____ There'll be
we need ____ is mu - sic, sweet mu - sic. ____ There'll be

mu - sic ev - 'ry - where. ____ } There'll be swing-ing, ____ sway-ing, and
mu - sic ev - 'ry - where. ____ }

rec - ords play - ing and danc - ing ____ in the street. ____ Oh, _____

____ it does - n't mat - ter _____ what you wear ____ just as

long as you are ____ there. _____ So come on, ____ ev -

- 'ry guy ____ grab a girl. ____ Ev - 'ry - where ____ a - round

the world ____ they'll be ____ danc - ing. ____

**D.S. al Coda**

They're danc - ing in the ___ street. _____ Ooh. This is an

**CODA**

danc - ing ___ in the street. Yeah. _____ *(Instrumental)*

Ah. Oh, it does - n't mat - ter what you wear _____ just ___

___ as long as you are there. _____ So come on, ___ ev -

- 'ry guy grab a girl. Ev - 'ry - where a - round

the world they'll be

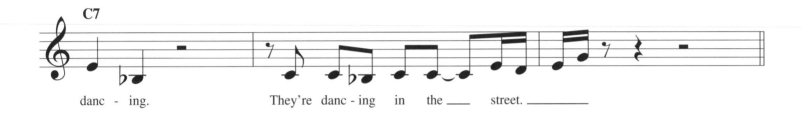

danc - ing. They're danc - ing in the street.

Phil - a - del - phia P. A., Bal - ti-more and D. C.

now, and if we get to that Mo - tor Cit - y, ah,

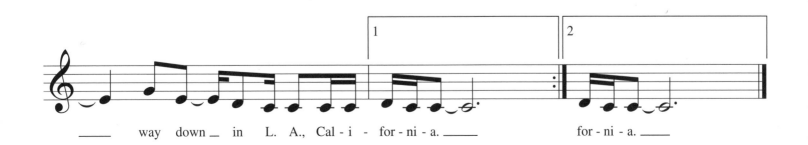

way down in L. A., Cal - i - for - ni - a. for - ni - a.

# DAYDREAM

Words and Music by
JOHN SEBASTIAN

# DEDICATED TO THE ONE I LOVE

Words and Music by LOWMAN PAULING
and RALPH BASS

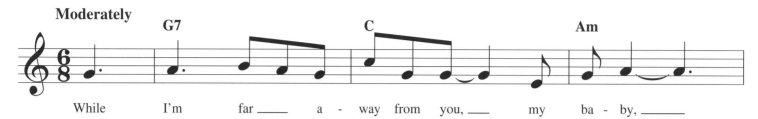

While I'm far a - way from you, ___ my ba - by, ___

I know ___ it's hard for you, my ba - by, ___

be - cause ___ it's hard for me, my ba - by. ___

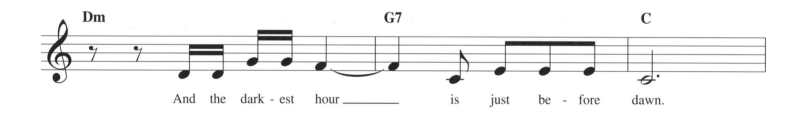

And the dark - est hour ___ is just be - fore dawn.

Each night be - fore ___ you go to bed, ___ } my
While I'm ___ far ___ a - way from you, ___ }

ba - by, ___ whis - per a lit - tle ___ prayer for me, my

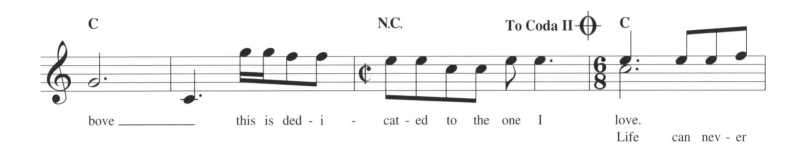

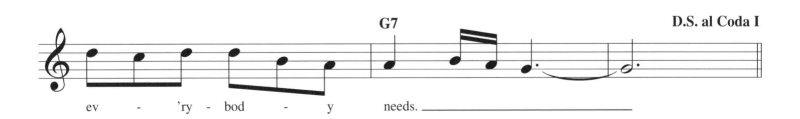

**CODA I**

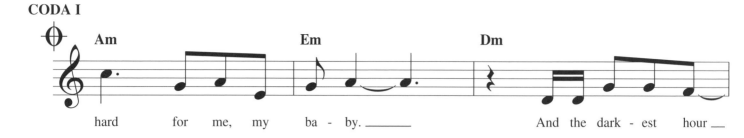

hard for me, my ba - by. _____ And the dark - est hour __

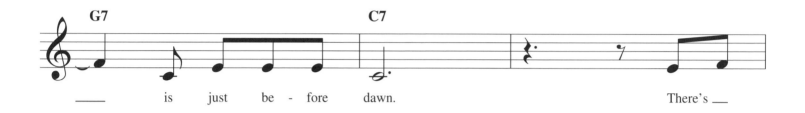

__ is just be - fore dawn. There's __

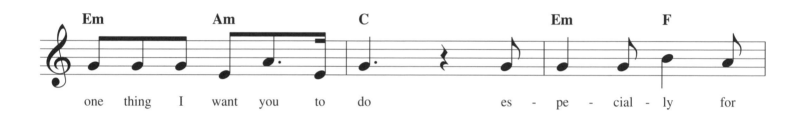

one thing I want you to do es - pe - cial - ly for

me. And it's some - thing _____ ev - 'ry - bod - y

**D.S. al Coda II**
**(Verse 1)**

**CODA II**

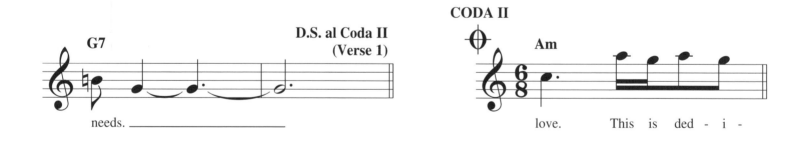

needs. _____ love. This is ded - i -

**Repeat and Fade**

cat - ed to the one I love. _____ This is ded - i -

# EARLY IN THE MORNING

Words and Music by MIKE LEANDER
and EDDIE SEAGO

# DO WAH DIDDY DIDDY

Words and Music by JEFF BARRY
and ELLIE GREENWICH

**Moderately**

There he was, _____ just a - walk - in' down the street, sing - in'
fore I knew _____ it he was walk - in' next to me, sing - in'

do    wah   did - dy did - dy,   down   did - dy   do.
do    wah   did - dy did - dy,   down   did - dy   do.      He

Pop - pin'  his  fin - gers  and  a - shuf - fl - in'  his  feet,  sing - in'
took   my   hand _____   just   as   nat - 'ral   as   can   be,   sing - in'

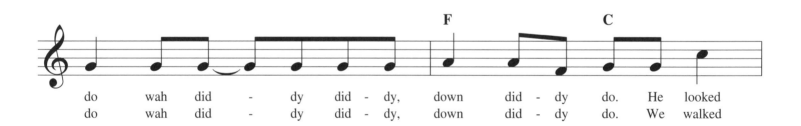

do   wah   did - dy   did - dy,   down   did - dy   do.  He  looked
do   wah   did - dy   did - dy,   down   did - dy   do.  We  walked

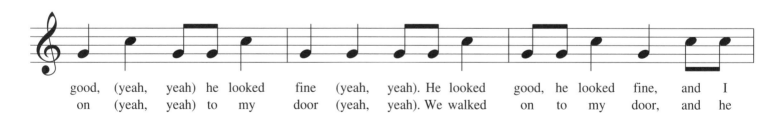

good, (yeah, yeah) he looked  fine  (yeah, yeah). He looked  good, he looked  fine,  and  I
on (yeah, yeah) to my  door  (yeah, yeah). We walked  on  to my  door,  and  he

near - ly  lost  my  mind.  Be -   stayed  a  lit - tle  more.        My,  my,  my,  my,      I

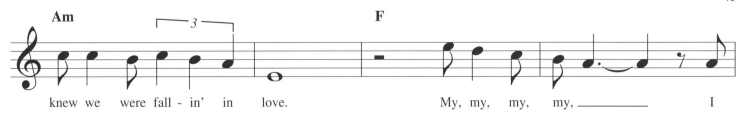

knew we were fall - in' in love. My, my, my, my, _____ I

told him all the things I was dream - in' of. _____ Now we're to - geth - er near - ly

ev - 'ry sin - gle day, sing - in' do wah did - dy did - dy, down did - dy do.

We're so hap - py and that's how we're gon - na stay, sing - in' do wah did - dy did - dy,

down did - dy do. 'Cause I'm his (yeah, yeah) and he's mine (yeah, yeah). Well, I'm

his and he's mine and the wed - din' bells will chime, sing - in' do wah did - dy did - dy,

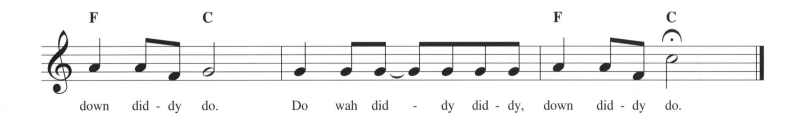

down did - dy do. Do wah did - dy did - dy, down did - dy do.

# DO YOU KNOW THE WAY TO SAN JOSE

Lyric by HAL DAVID
Music by BURT BACHARACH

**Moderately**

Do you know the way to San ___ Jo - se? I've been a - way so
You can real - ly breathe in San ___ Jo - se. They've got a lot of

long. I ___ may go wrong and lose ___ my way.
space. There'll ___ be a place where I ___ can stay.

Do you know the way to San ___ Jo - se? I'm go - ing back to
I was born and raised in San ___ Jo - se. I'm go - ing back to

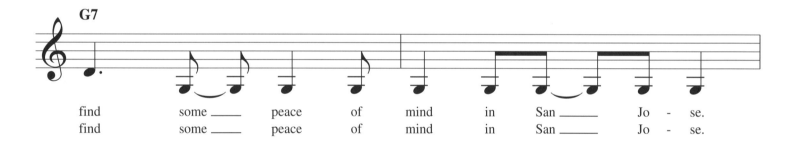

find some ___ peace of mind in San ___ Jo - se.
find some ___ peace of mind in San ___ Jo - se.

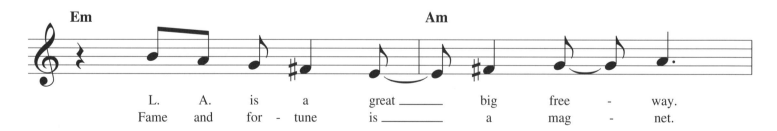

L. A. is a great ___ big free - way.
Fame and for - tune is ___ a mag - net.

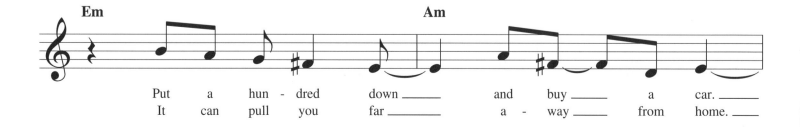

Put a hun - dred down ___ and buy ___ a car.
It can pull you far ___ a - way ___ from home. ___

**Em**                          **Dm**

_____ In a week, may - be two, they'll make ___ you a
_____ With a dream in your heart you're nev - er a -

**G**     **Dm**                    **G**

star. Weeks turn in - to years. How quick ___ they pass, ___
lone. Dreams turn in - to dust and blow ___ a - way, ___

**N.C.**                    **G7**

_____ and all the stars _____ that nev - er were ___
_____ and there you are _____ with - out a friend. ___

_____ are park - ing cars ___ and pump - ing gas. _____
_____ You pack your car ___ and ride ___ a - way. _____

**C**                  **F**                    **C**

I've got lots of friends in San ___ Jo - se. *(Instrumental)*

                                          **F**

Do you know the way to San ___ Jo - se?
Can't wait to get back to San ___ Jo - se.

**C**

*(Instrumental)*

# DON'T LET THE SUN CATCH YOU CRYING

Words and Music by GERARD MARSDEN,
FRED MARSDEN, LES CHADWICK and LES MAGUIRE

**With an easy flow**

Don't let the sun catch you cry - ing, ___

the night's the time for all your tears. ___

___ Your heart may be bro - ken to - night,

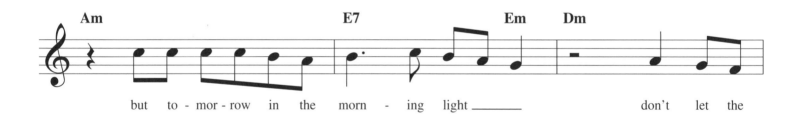

but to - mor - row in the morn - ing light ___ don't let the

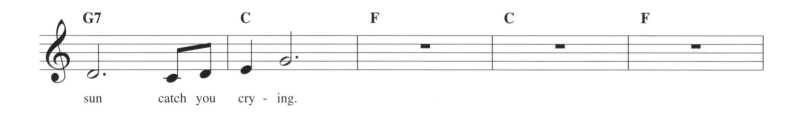

sun catch you cry - ing.

The night - time shad - ows ___ dis - ap - pear ___
It may be hard ___ to dis - cov - er ___

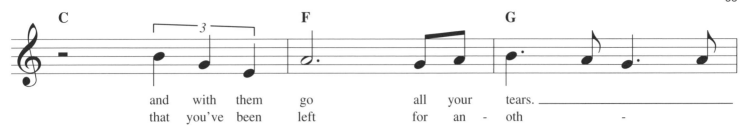

and with them go all your tears. _____
that you've been left for an - oth -

_____ For the morn - ing will bring joy for
er. But don't for - get that life's a game and it can

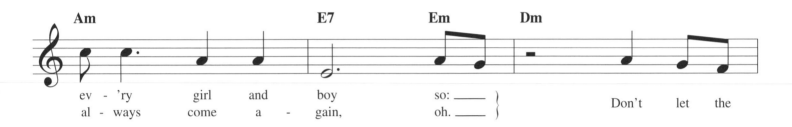

ev - 'ry girl and boy so: _____ }
al - ways come a - gain, oh. _____ }    Don't let the

**To Coda** ⊕

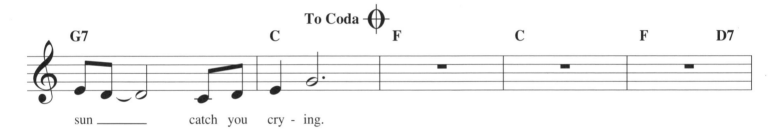

sun _____ catch you cry - ing.

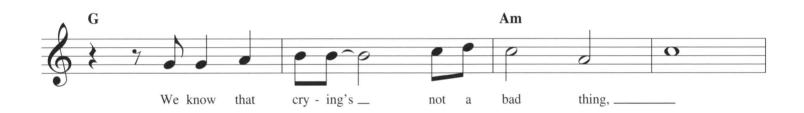

We know that cry - ing's _____ not a bad thing, _____

**D.S. al Coda**

but stop your cry - ing ____ when the birds sing. _____

**CODA** ⊕

Don't let the sun catch you cry - ing, oh no, oh - oh - oh.

# DOWNTOWN

Words and Music by
TONY HATCH

**Medium Rock**

When you're a - lone ___ and life is mak - ing you lone - ly, you can
Don't hang a - round ___ and let your prob - lems sur - round ___ you, there are
*Instrumental*

al - ways go _____ down - town. When you've got wor - ries, all the
mov - ie shows ___ down - town. May - be you know ___ some lit - tle

noise and the hur - ry seems to help, I know. ___ Down - town. Just
plac - es to go ___ to where they nev - er close. ___ Down - town. Just
*End instrumental* And

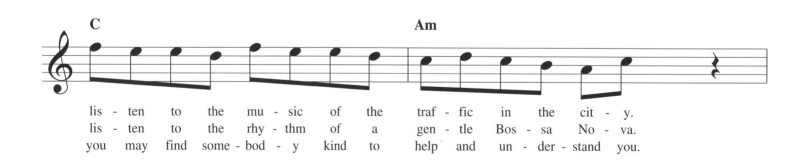

lis - ten to the mu - sic of the traf - fic in the cit - y.
lis - ten to the rhy - thm of a gen - tle Bos - sa No - va.
you may find some - bod - y kind to help and un - der - stand you.

Lin - ger on the side - walk where the ne - on signs are pret - ty.
You'll be danc - ing with 'em too be - fore the night is o - ver,
Some - one who is just like you and needs a gen - tle hand to

# EVE OF DESTRUCTION

Words and Music by P.F. SLOAN
and STEVE BARRI

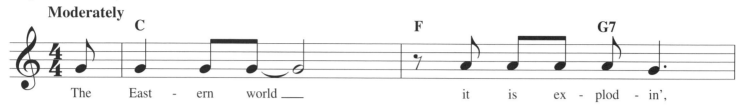

The East-ern world ___ it is ex-plod-in',

vi-o-lence flar-in' and bul-lets load-in'. You're

old e-nough to kill, but not for ___ vot-in'. You

don't be-lieve in war, but what's that gun you're tot-in'? And

e-ven the Jor-dan Riv-er has bod-ies float-in'! But you

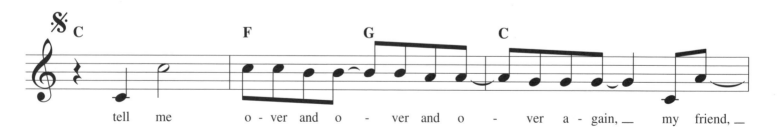

tell me o-ver and o-ver and o-ver a-gain, ___ my friend, ___

___ ah, you don't be-lieve we're on the eve ___ of des-

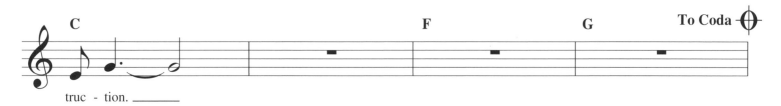

To Coda

truc - tion. _____

Don't you un - der - stand what I'm try'n' to say? __ Can't you feel the fear _____ that I'm

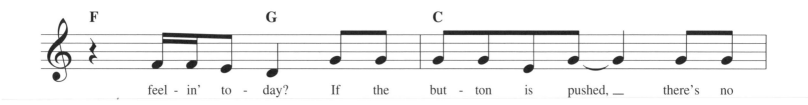

feel - in' to - day? If the but - ton is pushed, __ there's no

run - ning a - way. _____ There'll be no one to save _____ with the

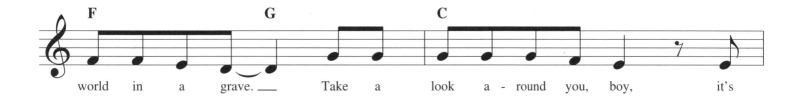

world in a grave. __ Take a look a - round you, boy, it's

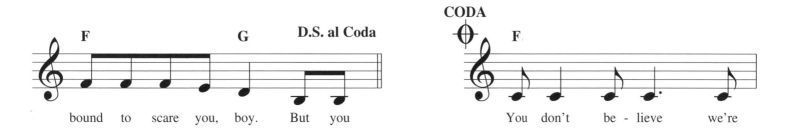

D.S. al Coda          CODA

bound to scare you, boy. But you          You don't be - lieve we're

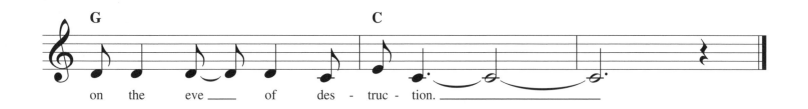

on the eve ___ of des - truc - tion. _____

# FOR ONCE IN MY LIFE

Words by RONALD MILLER
Music by ORLANDO MURDEN

**Slowly, with feeling**

For once in my life I have some - one who needs me,

some - one I've need - ed so long. For once, un - a - fraid I can

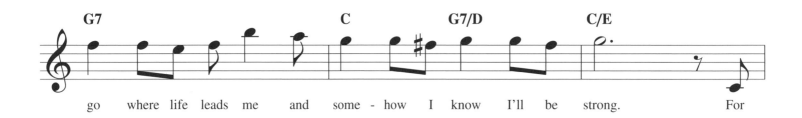

go where life leads me and some - how I know I'll be strong. For

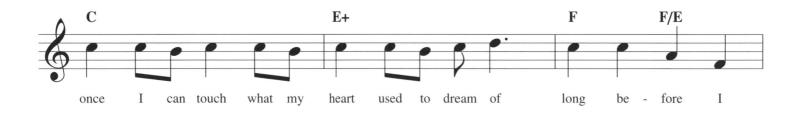

once I can touch what my heart used to dream of long be - fore I

knew some - one warm like you would make my dream come

true. For once in my life I won't let sor - row hurt me,

not like it's hurt me be - fore. For once I have some - thing I

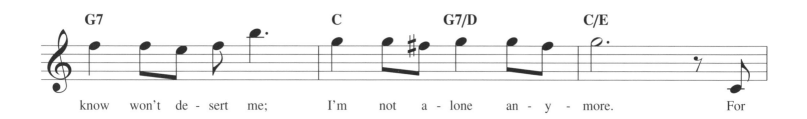

know won't de - sert me; I'm not a - lone an - y - more. For

once I can say this is mine, you can't take it, long as I know I have

love, I can make it. For once in my life I have some - one who needs

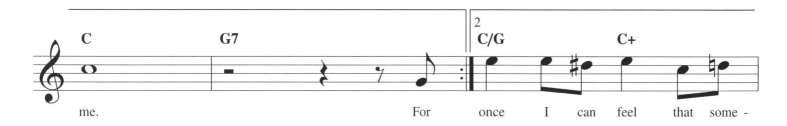

me. For once I can feel that some -

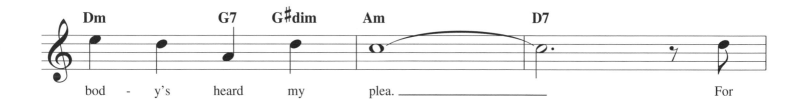

bod - y's heard my plea. For

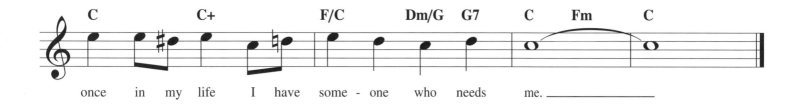

once in my life I have some - one who needs me.

# GENTLE ON MY MIND

Words and Music by
JOHN HARTFORD

# GREEN ONIONS

Written by AL JACKSON, JR., LEWIS STEINBERG,
BOOKER T. JONES and STEVE CROPPER

# THE GIRL FROM IPANEMA
### (Garôta De Ipanema)

Music by ANTONIO CARLOS JOBIM
English Words by NORMAN GIMBEL
Original Words by VINICIUS DE MORAES

**Moderate Bossa Nova**

Tall      and    tan    and     young    and  love  -  ly,   the
When    she  walks  she's   like    a     sam  -  ba   that

girl    from    I    -  pa  -  ne  -  ma   goes      walk  - ing,   and
swings  so    cool   and    sways _____      so    gen - tle,   that

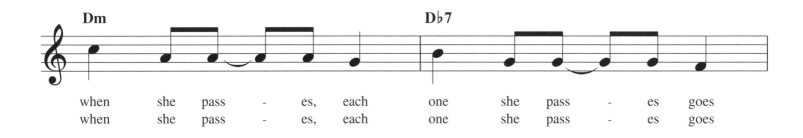

when    she   pass  -  es,   each    one    she   pass  -   es    goes
when    she   pass  -  es,   each    one    she   pass  -   es    goes

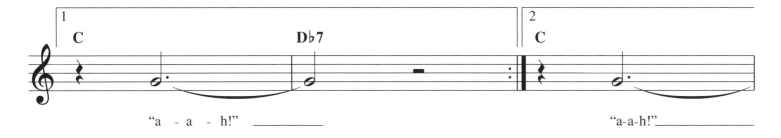

1
C                                    Db7

"a - a - h!" _____

2
C

"a - a - h!" _____

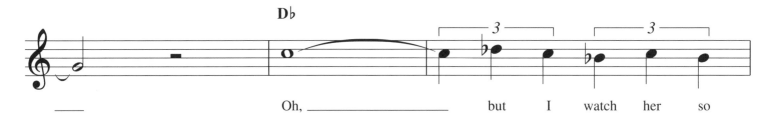

Db

Oh, _____            but    I   watch   her   so

Gb7                                              C#m

sad  -  ly. _____                                    How _____

# GOIN' OUT OF MY HEAD

Words and Music by TEDDY RANDAZZO
and BOBBY WEINSTEIN

**Moderately slow Rock**

Well, I think I'm go - in' out of my head. Yes, I
think I'm go - in' out of my head, 'cause I

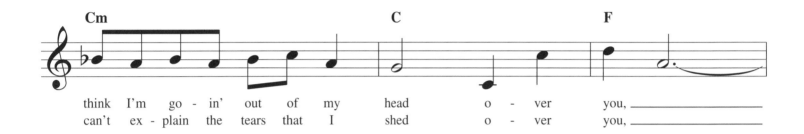

think I'm go - in' out of my head o - ver you, _____
can't ex - plain the tears that I shed o - ver you, _____

_____ o - ver you. _____ I
_____ o - ver you. _____ I

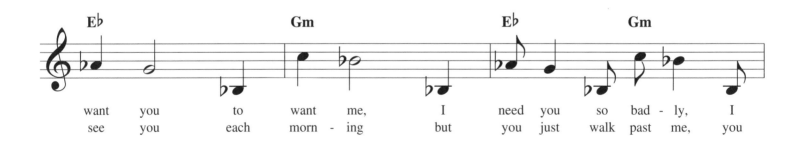

want you to want me, I need you so bad - ly, I
see you each morn - ing but you just walk past me, you

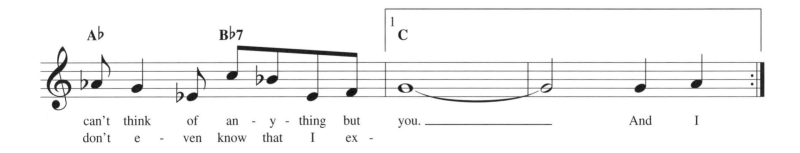

can't think of an - y - thing but you. _____ And I
don't e - ven know that I ex -

65

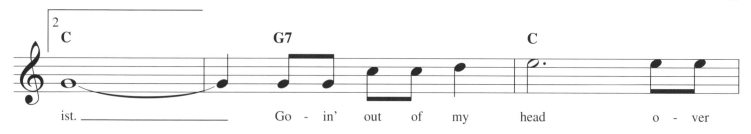

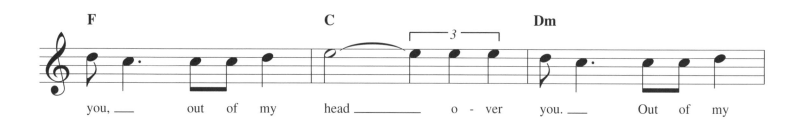

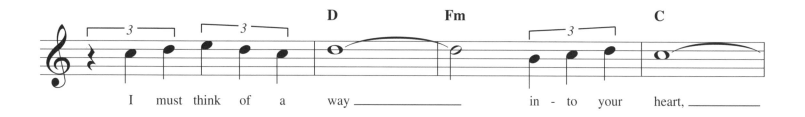

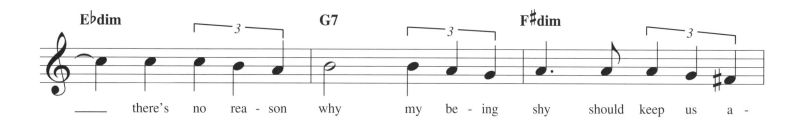

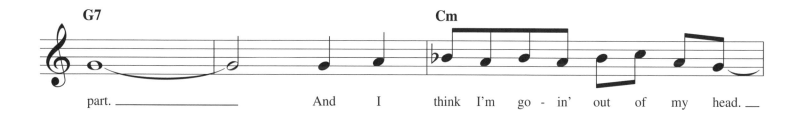

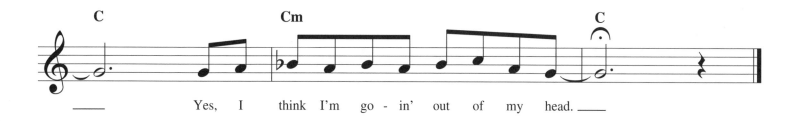

# GOOD VIBRATIONS

Words and Music by BRIAN WILSON
and MIKE LOVE

**Light Rock**

I, _____
Close my eyes.
I love the col - or - ful clothes she wears, _____
She's some - how clos - er now. _____

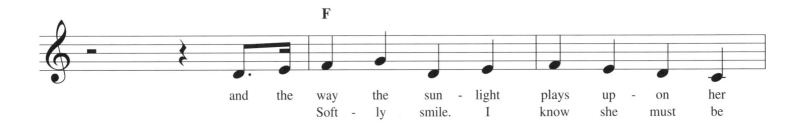

and the way the sun - light plays up - on her
Soft - ly smile. I know she must be

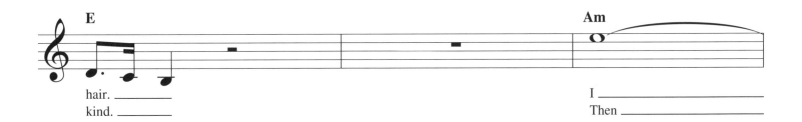

hair. _____
kind. _____
I _____
Then _____

_____ hear the sound of a gen - tle word, _____
_____ I look in her eyes. _____
on _____ the
She _____ goes

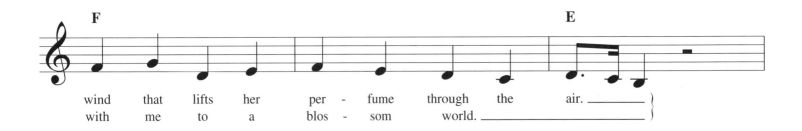

wind that lifts her per - fume through the air. _____
with me to a blos - som world. _____

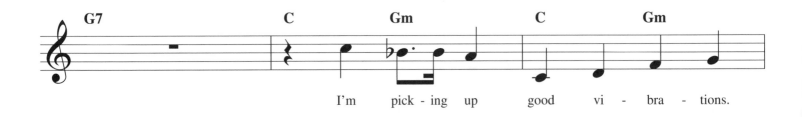

I'm pick - ing up good vi - bra - tions.

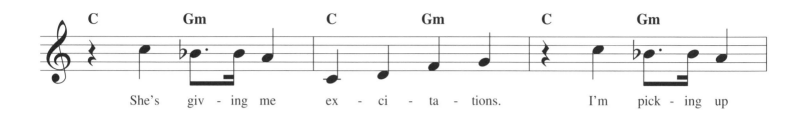

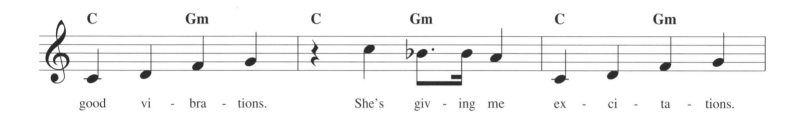

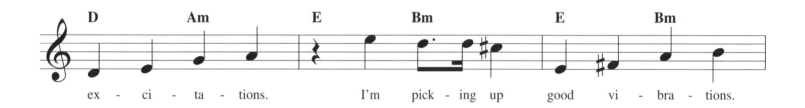

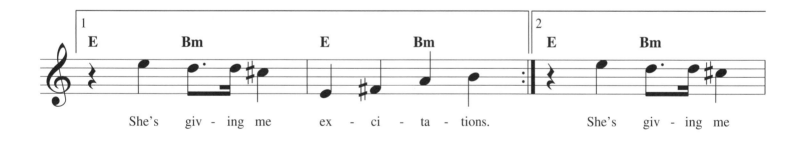

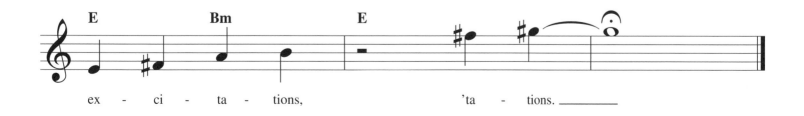

# GREENFIELDS

Words and Music by TERRY GILKYSON,
RICHARD DEHR and FRANK MILLER

**Slowly, with a steady beat**

noth - ing   in  this   wide   world   left  for   me   to  see,   but   I'll ____ keep  on  wait - in'

'til ____ you  re - turn.   I'll ____ keep  on  wait - ing   un - til   the  day   you  learn

you can't   be hap - py   while   your heart's on   the roam.   You can't   be hap - py   un -

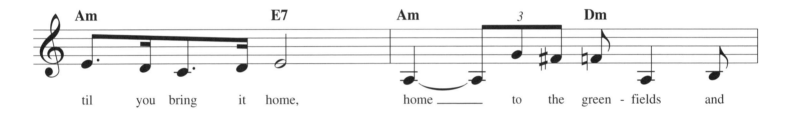

til   you  bring   it  home,   home ____ to   the  green - fields   and

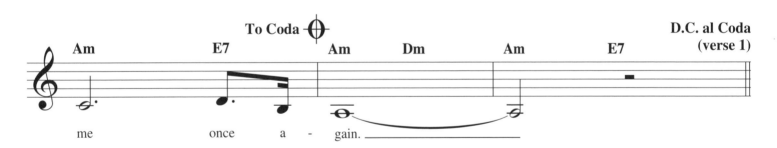

me   once   a - gain. _____

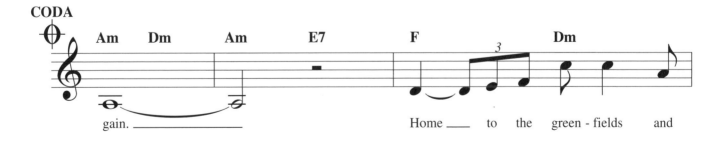

gain. _____   Home ___ to   the  green - fields   and

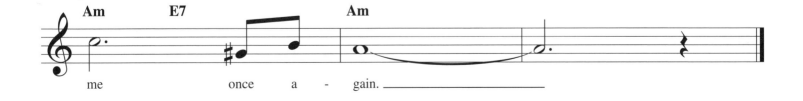

me   once   a - gain. _____

# A GROOVY KIND OF LOVE

Words and Music by TONI WINE
and CAROLE BAYER SAGER

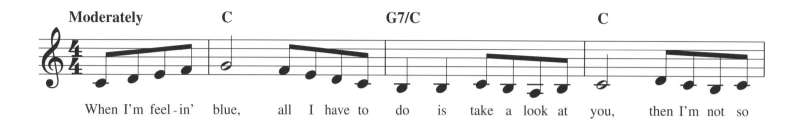

When I'm feel-in' blue, all I have to do is take a look at you, then I'm not so

blue. When you're close to me I can feel your heart beat I can hear you breath-ing in my

ear. Would-n't you a - gree, ba - by, you and me got a groov-y kind of

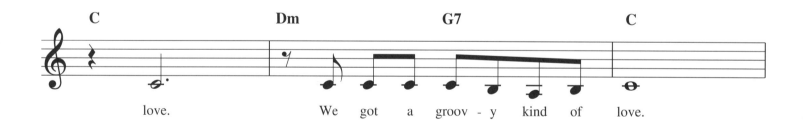

love. We got a groov-y kind of love.

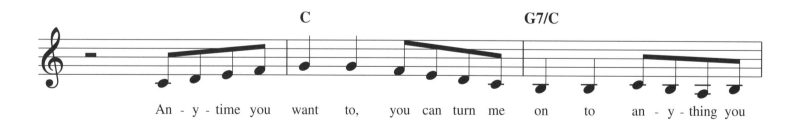

An - y-time you want to, you can turn me on to an - y-thing you

want to, an - y-time at all. When I taste your lips, oh, I start to

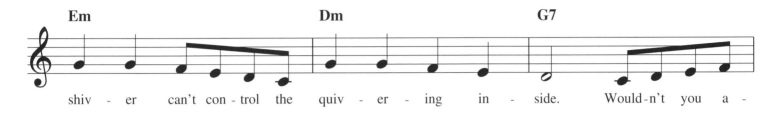

shiv - er can't con - trol the quiv - er - ing in - side. Would -n't you a -

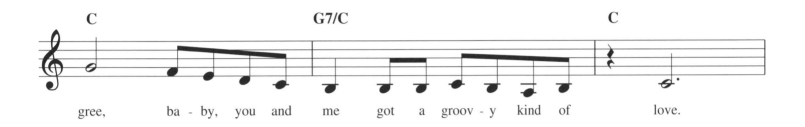

gree, ba - by, you and me got a groov - y kind of love.

We got a groov - y kind of love. *(Instrumental)*

When I'm in your arms noth - ing seems to mat - ter if the world would

shat - ter I don't care. Would -n't you a - gree, ba - by, you and

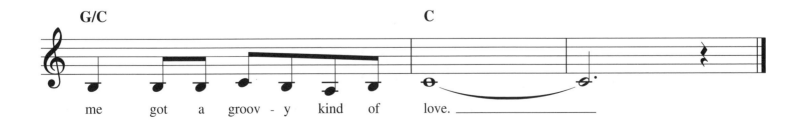

me got a groov - y kind of love. _____

# HAPPY TOGETHER

Words and Music by GARRY BONNER
and ALAN GORDON

I - mag - ine me and you.____ I do.    I think a - bout you
call you up.____ In - vest a dime and you say you be -

day and night,____ it's on - ly right    to think a - bout the
long to me ____ and ease my mind,    i - mag - ine how the

girl you love,____ and hold her tight,    so hap - py to -
world would be ____ so ver - y fine,    so hap - py to -

geth - er. ____                    If I should    geth - er. ____

I can see me lov - in' no - bod - y but you for all my life. ___

73

# HELP ME RHONDA

Words and Music by BRIAN WILSON
and MIKE LOVE

Since she put me down I've been out___ do - in' in my head. ___
gon - na be my wife and I was gon - na be her man. ___

Come in late at night__ and in the morn - in' I just lay in bed. __
But she let an - oth - er guy come be - tween us and it shat - tered our plans. __

Well, Rhon - da, you look ___ so fine, ____ and I
Well, Rhon - da, you caught ___ my eye, ____ and I'll

know it would - n't take much time ____ for you to { help me, Rhon - da,
give you lots of rea - sons why ____ you got - ta {

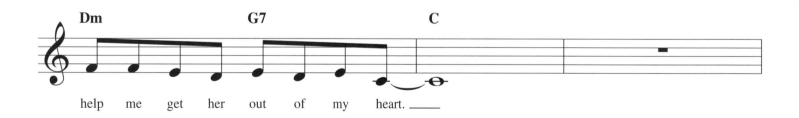

help me get her out of my heart. ___

Help me, Rhon - da! Help, help me, Rhon - da! Help me, Rhon - da!

# HEY JUDE

Words and Music by JOHN LENNON
and PAUL McCARTNEY

Hey Jude, don't make it bad. Take a
sad song and make it bet - ter. Re -
mem - ber to let her in - to your heart. Then you can start
to make it bet - ter. (Hey)

Jude, don't be a - fraid. You were made to go out and
Jude, don't let me down. You have found her, now go and

get her. The min - ute you let her un - der your
get her. Re - mem - ber to let her in - to your

skin. Then you be - gin to make it bet - ter.
heart. Then you can start to make it bet - ter.

And an-y-time you feel the pain, hey Jude, __ re-frain, ___ don't car-ry the world __
So let it out and let it in, hey Jude, __ be-gin, _____ you're wait-ing for some -

_____ up - on your shoul - ders. For well you know that it's a
- one to per - form ___ with. And don't you know that it's just

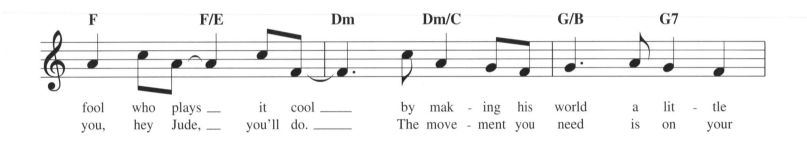

fool who plays ___ it cool _____ by mak - ing his world a lit - tle
you, hey Jude, __ you'll do. _____ The move - ment you need is on your

cold - er, da da da da da da da da da
shoul - der, da da da da da da da da da

**D.S. al Coda**
**(Second time)**

**CODA**

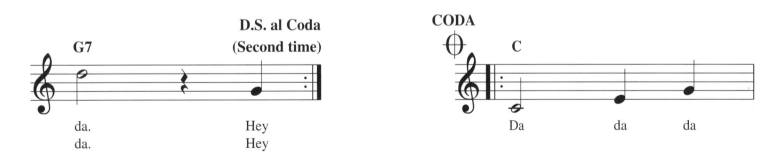

da. Hey
da. Hey

Da da da

da da da da da da da da, Hey ___ Jude.

# HONEY

Words and Music by
BOBBY RUSSELL

**Moderately**

1. See the tree, how big it's grown? But friend, it has-n't been too long, it
2. Then the first snow came and she ran out to brush the snow a-way so it
3.-8. *(See additional lyrics)*

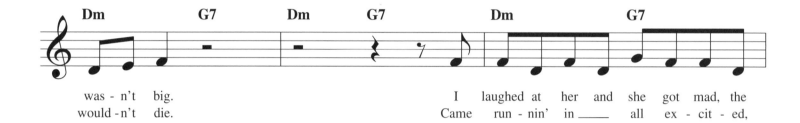

was-n't big.                                    I laughed at her and she got mad, the
would-n't die.                                  Came run-nin' in _____ all ex-cit-ed,

first day that she plant-ed it was just a twig.
slipped and al-most hurt her-self, I laughed 'til I cried.

|1, 3, 5, 7|

|2, 4, 6, 8|

**Chorus**

And Hon-ey, I miss you,

and I'm be-ing good. _____                And I'd love to be

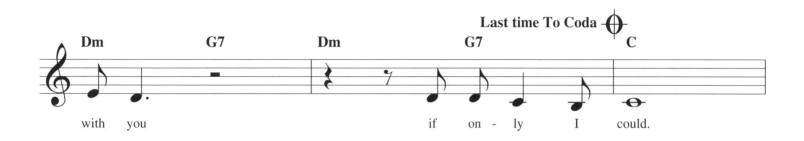

with    you                                                    if    on - ly    I    could.

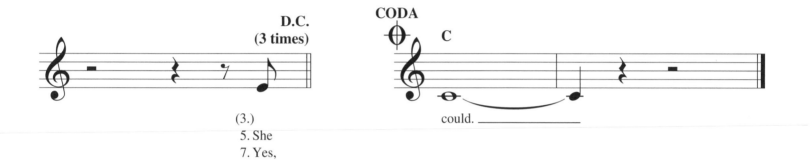

(3.)
5. She
7. Yes,

*Additional Lyrics*

3. She was always young at heart,
   Kinda dumb and kinda smart and I loved her so.
   I surprised her with a puppy;
   Kept me up all Christmas eve two years ago.

4. And it would sure embarrass her
   When I came home from working late 'cause I would know
   That she'd been sittin' there and cryin'
   Over some sad and silly late, late show.
   *Chorus*

5. She wrecked the car and she was sad
   And so afraid that I'd be mad, but what the heck.
   Tho' I pretended hard to be, guess you could say
   She saw through me and hugged my neck.

6. I came home unexpectedly and
   Found her crying needlessly in the middle of the day,
   And it was in the early Spring
   When flowers bloom and robins sing she went away.
   *Chorus*

7. Yes, one day while I wasn't home
   While she was there and all alone the angels came.
   Now all I have is memories of Honey,
   And I wake up nights and call her name.

8. Now my life's an empty stage
   Where Honey lived and Honey played and love grew up.
   A small cloud passes overhead and
   Cries down in the flower bed that Honey loved.
   *Chorus*

# HURT SO BAD

Words and Music by TEDDY RANDAZZO,
BOBBY WEINSTEIN and BOBBY HART

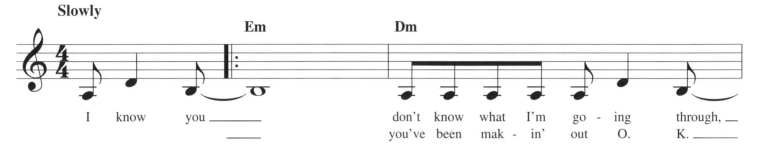

I know you _____ don't know what I'm go - ing through, _____
_____ you've been mak - in' out O. K. _____

____ stand - ing here _____ look - ing at you. _____
____ She's in love; _____ don't stand in her way. _____

_____ Well, let me tell you that it hurt so bad. _____
_____ But let me tell you that it hurt so bad. _____

_____ It makes me feel so bad. _____
_____ It makes me feel so bad. _____

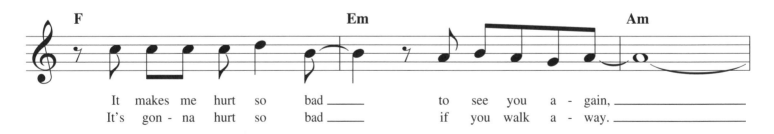

It makes me hurt so bad _____ to see you a - gain, _____
It's gon - na hurt so bad _____ if you walk a - way. _____

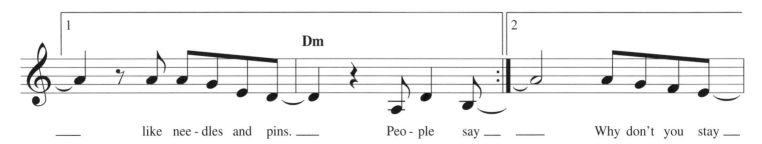

____ like nee - dles and pins. _____ Peo - ple say __ ____ Why don't you stay _____

and let me make it up to you? _____ Stay, I'll do an-y-thing you

want me to. _____ You loved me be-fore, __ please love me a-gain. __ I

can't let you go back to him. Please don't go, please don't go. It hurt so bad. __

_____ Come back, it hurt so bad. _____

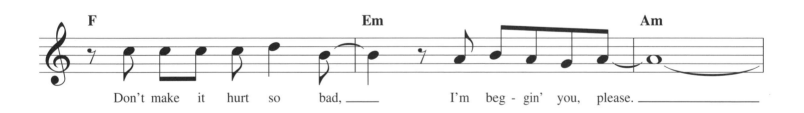

Don't make it hurt so bad, _____ I'm beg-gin' you, please. _____

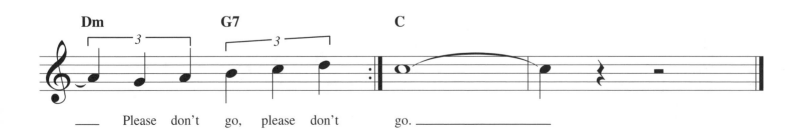

___ Please don't go, please don't go. _____

# I CAN'T HELP MYSELF
### (Sugar Pie, Honey Bunch)

Words and Music by BRIAN HOLLAND,
LAMONT DOZIER and EDWARD HOLLAND

**Moderately fast**

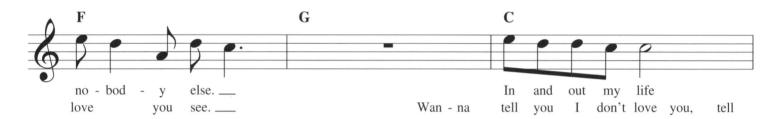

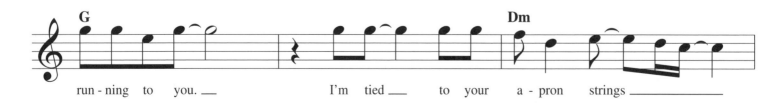

and there's noth-ing ___ that I can do. ___ *(Instrumental)*

Can't help my-self, ___ no, ___ I can't help my-self.

**D.C. al Coda**

**CODA**

___ I call your name, girl, ___ it starts the flame burn-

-ing in my heart, tear-ing it all a-part, No mat-ter how I try, my love ___

___ I can-not hide. 'Cause sug-ar pie, hon-ey bunch, you know that I'm
Sug-ar pie, hon-ey bunch, do an-y-thing you

weak for you. ___ Can't help my-self, ___
ask me to. ___ Can't help my-self, ___

I love ___ you and no-bod-y else.
I want ___ you and no-bod-y else.

# I GET AROUND

Words and Music by BRIAN WILSON
and MIKE LOVE

**Medium bright Rock**

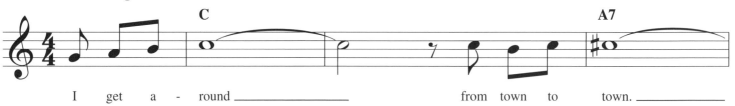

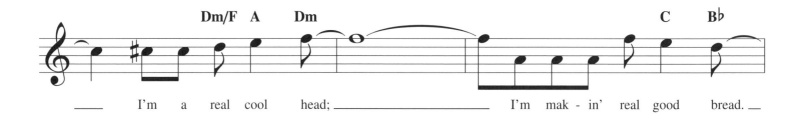

I get a - round _____ from town to town. _____

_____ I'm a real cool head; _____ I'm mak - in' real good bread. _____

_____ I'm get - tin' bugged, driv - in' up an' down the
al - ways take my car ____ 'cause it's

same ol' strip. ____ I got - ta find a new place where the
nev - er been beat, ____ and ____ we've nev - er missed yet with the

G7    N.C.

kids are hip. ___ *(Instrumental)*
girls we meet. ___

{ My
{ None of the

bud - dies and me ____ are get - tin' real well - known, ___ yeah, the
guys ____ go stead - y 'cause it would - n't be right ____ to leave your

bad guys know us and they leave us a - lone. ____ } I get a -
best girl home ____ on a Sat - ur - day night. ____ }

round _____ from town to town. _____

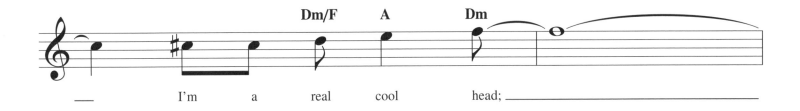

____ I'm a real cool head; _____

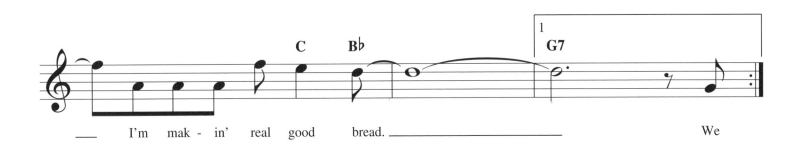

____ I'm mak - in' real good bread. _____ We

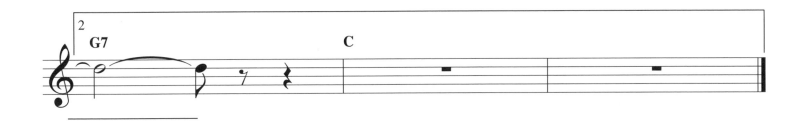

# I HEARD IT THROUGH THE GRAPEVINE

Words and Music by NORMAN J. WHITFIELD
amd BARRETT STRONG

**Moderately**

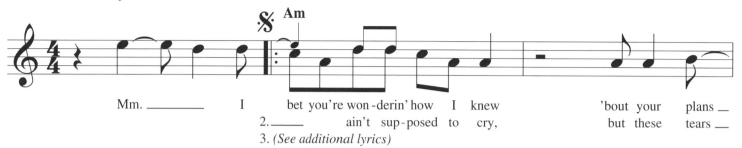

Mm. _____ I bet you're won-derin' how I knew 'bout your plans _____
2. _____ ain't sup-posed to cry, but these tears _____
3. (See additional lyrics)

_____ to make me blue, _____ with some oth-er guy _____ you knew be-fore.
_____ I can't hold in-side. _____ Los-in' you _____ would end my life you see,

Be-tween the two of us guys _____ you know I loved you more. _____ It took me by sur-
'cause you mean _____ that much to me. _____ You could have told _

prise _____ I must say _____ when I found out yes-ter-day. _
me your-self _____ that you loved _ some-one else. _

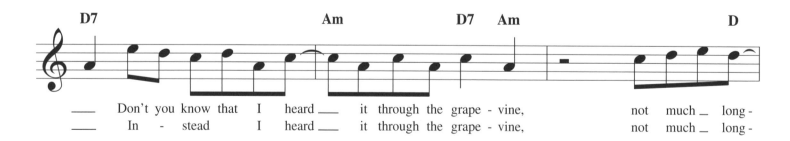

_____ Don't you know that I heard _____ it through the grape-vine, not much _ long-
_____ In-stead I heard _____ it through the grape-vine, not much _ long-

-er would you be _____ mine. Uh huh, heard it through the grape-vine.
-er would you be _____ mine. Oh, I heard _____ it through the grape-vine.

**D7**

Oh, ___ I'm just a-bout to lose _____ my mind. ___ Hon-ey, hon-ey oh
And I'm just a-bout to lose _____ my mind. ___ (I

**Am**　　　　　　　　　　　　　　　　　　　　　　　　**To Coda** ⊕

yeah.
heard it through the grape-vine, not much long-er would you be mine, ba - by.) ⎰ Ooh. ___
　　　　　　　　　　　　　　　　　　　　　　　　　　　　　⎨ Ooh. ___
　　　　　　　　　　　　　　　　　　　　　　　　　　　　　⎱ Yeah. ___

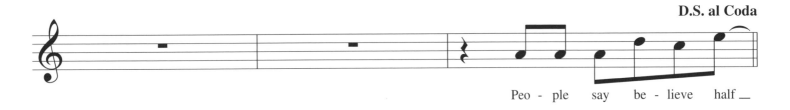

|1|　　|2|

_____ I know a man ___ _____ Ooh. _____

**D.S. al Coda**

Peo - ple say be - lieve half ___

**CODA** ⊕

___ yeah, yeah, ___ yeah. I heard it through the grape - vine, not much

long - er would you be mine, ba - by. Yeah. ___ - by.

*Additional Lyrics*

3. People say believe half of what you see
　Oh, and none of what you hear;
　But I can't help but be confused
　If it's true please tell me dear.
　Do you plan to let me go
　For the other guy you loved before?

# I WANT TO HOLD YOUR HAND

Words and Music by JOHN LENNON
and PAUL McCARTNEY

**Moderately, with a beat**

Oh yeah, I'll _____ tell you some - thing      I think you'll un - der -
please _____ say to me _____      you'll let me be your

stand.      When I _____ say that some - thing,
man,      and please _____ say to me _____

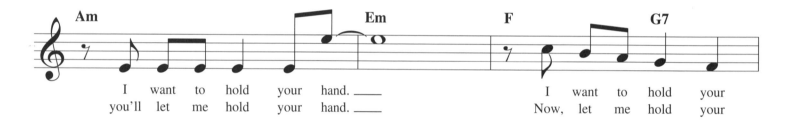

I want to hold your hand. ____      I want to hold your
you'll let me hold your hand. ____      Now, let me hold your

hand, _____      I want to hold your hand.   Oh ___
hand, _____

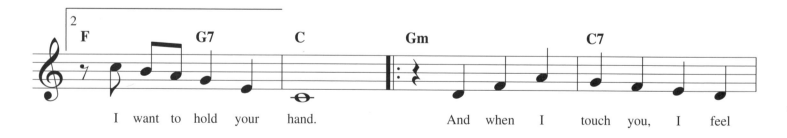

I want to hold your hand.      And when I touch you, I feel

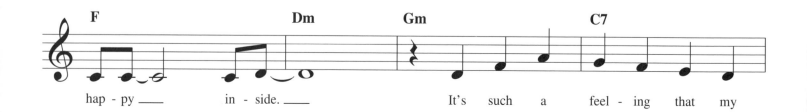

hap - py ___ in - side. ___      It's such a feel - ing that my

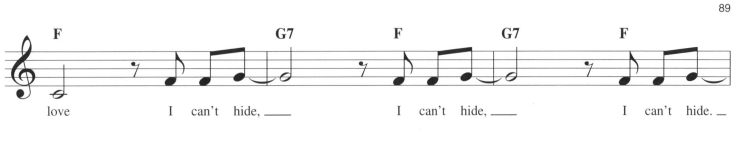

love  I can't hide, ____  I can't hide, ____  I can't hide. __

____  Yeah, you ____  got that

some - thing, I think you'll un - der - stand. When

I ____ { say / feel } that some - thing, I want to hold your hand, __

____ I want to hold your hand, _____

I want to hold your hand.  I want to hold your

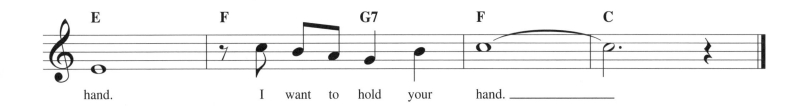

hand.  I want to hold your hand. ____

# I WILL FOLLOW HIM
## (I Will Follow You)

English Words by NORMAN GIMBEL and ARTHUR ALTMAN
French Words by JACQUES PLANTE
Music by J.W. STOLE and DEL ROMA

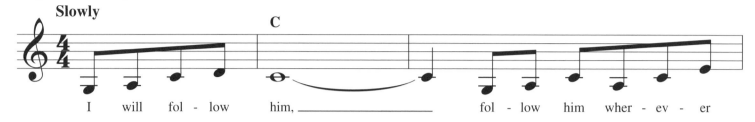

I will fol - low him, _____ fol - low him wher - ev - er

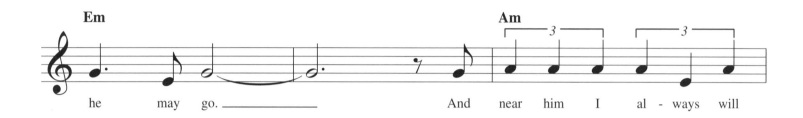

he may go. _____ And near him I al - ways will

be, for noth - ing can keep me a - way. He is my

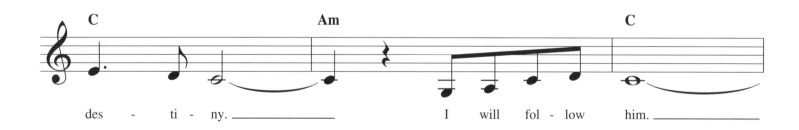

des - ti - ny. _____ I will fol - low him. _____

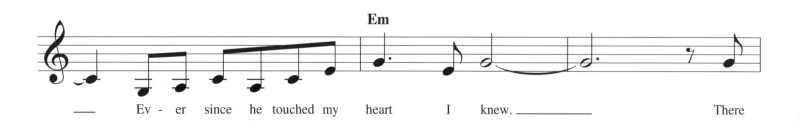

_____ Ev - er since he touched my heart I knew. _____ There

91

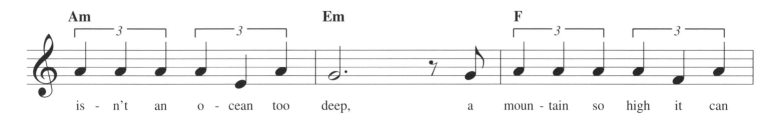

is - n't an o - cean too deep, a moun - tain so high it can

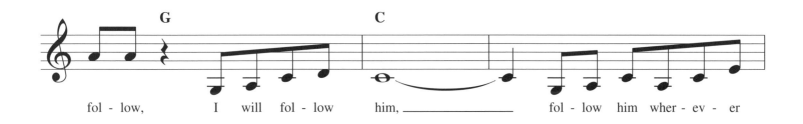

keep, keep me a - way, _____ a - way from his love. _____

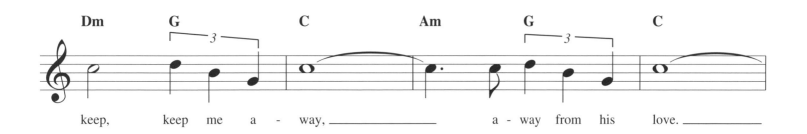

_____ (Instrumental)

I

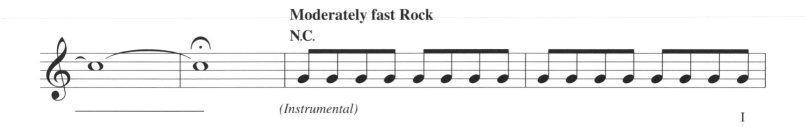

love him, I love him, I love him. And where he goes I'll fol - low, I'll fol - low, I'll

fol - low, I will fol - low him, _____ fol - low him wher - ev - er

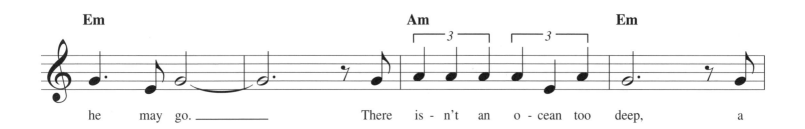

he may go. _____ There is - n't an o - cean too deep, a

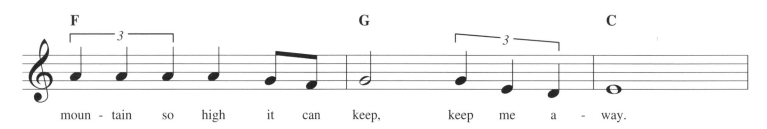

mountain so high it can keep, keep me a - way.

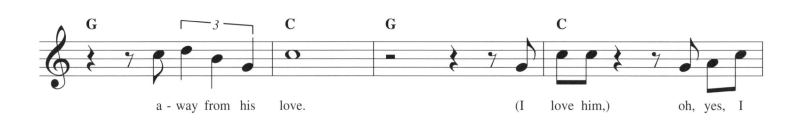

I will fol - low him, _____ fol - low him wher - ev - er

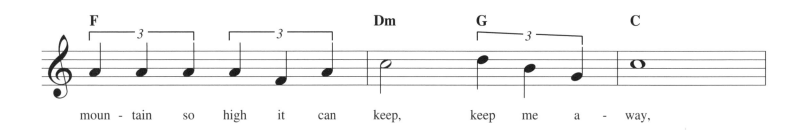

he may go. _____ There is - n't an o - cean too deep, a

moun - tain so high it can keep, keep me a - way,

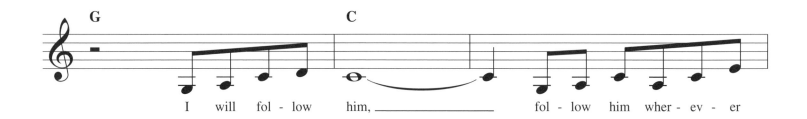

a - way from his love. (I love him,) oh, yes, I

love _____ him. (I'll fol - low,) I'm gon - na fol - low. _____

True love, he'll al-ways be my true ___ love. (For - ev - er,) from now un - til for -

ev - er. ___ I love him, I love him, I love him. And where he goes I'll

fol - low, I'll fol - low, I'll fol - low. He'll al - ways be my true love, my true love, my

true love from now un - til for - ev - er, for - ev - er, for - ev - er. ___ There

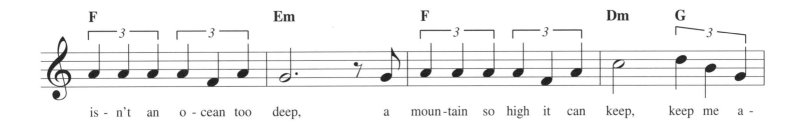

is - n't an o - cean too deep, a moun-tain so high it can keep, keep me a -

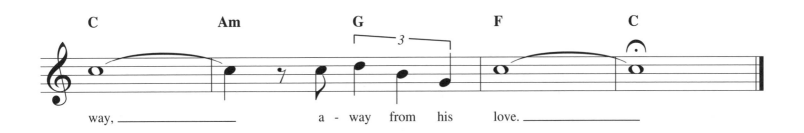

way, ___ a - way from his love. ___

# I WISH YOU LOVE

English Words by ALBERT BEACH
French Words and Music by CHARLES TRENET

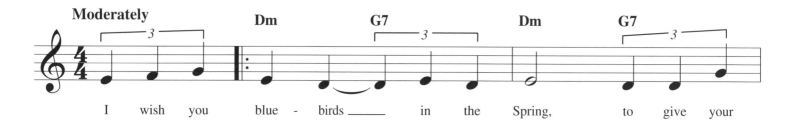

I wish you blue - birds ___ in the Spring, to give your

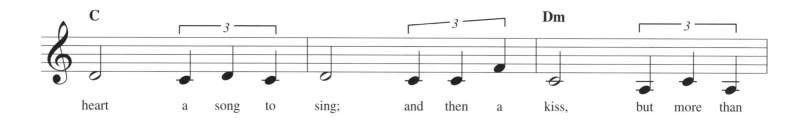

heart a song to sing; and then a kiss, but more than

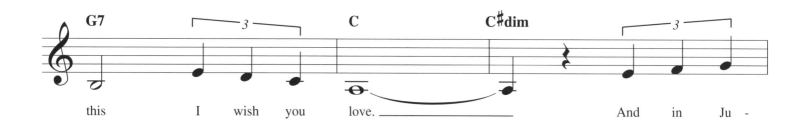

this I wish you love. ___ And in Ju -

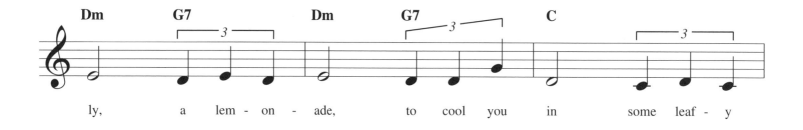

ly, a lem - on - ade, to cool you in some leaf - y

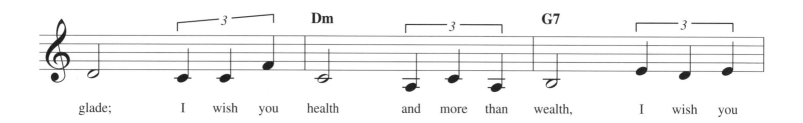

glade; I wish you health and more than wealth, I wish you

love. ___ My break - ing heart and I a -

gree     that   you   and   I     could   nev - er   be,     so   with   my

best,     my   ver - y   best,     I   set   you     free. _____

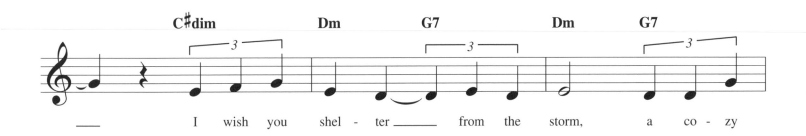

___     I   wish   you   shel - ter ___ from   the   storm,     a   co - zy

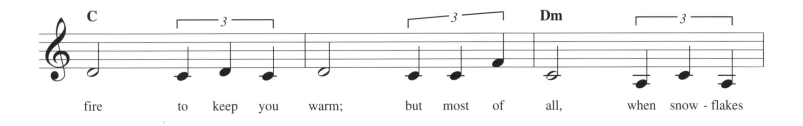

fire     to   keep   you   warm;     but   most   of   all,     when   snow - flakes

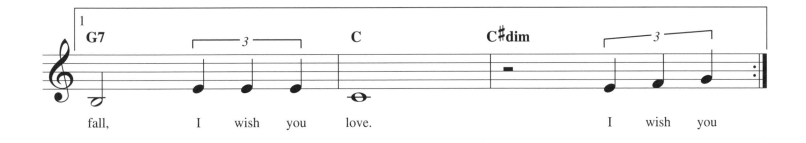

fall,     I   wish   you   love.     I   wish   you

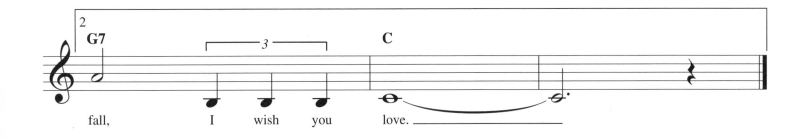

fall,     I   wish   you   love. _____

# I'M SORRY

Words and Music by RONNIE SELF
and DUB ALBRITTEN

**Slowly**

I'm sor - ry, so sor - ry that I was ____ such a fool. _

I did - n't know _ love could be so cruel.

You tell me mis - takes ____ are part of ____ be - ing young. _ But

that does - n't right _ the wrong that's been done. I'm sor - ry,

so sor - ry; please ac - cept my ____ a - pol - o - gy. _ But love is ____ blind _ and

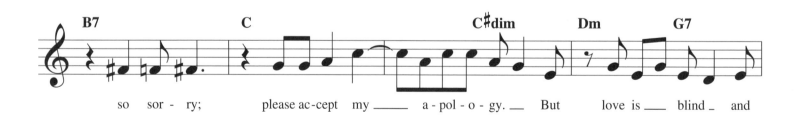

I was too blind to see. see. ____

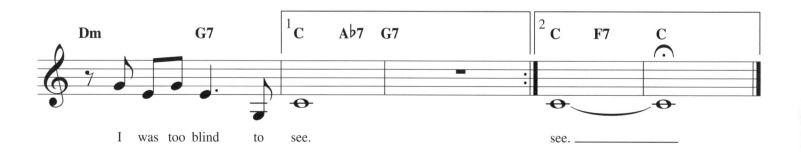

# IF I HAD A HAMMER
## (The Hammer Song)

Words and Music by LEE HAYS
and PETE SEEGER

*Additional Lyrics*

3. If I had a song,
   I'd sing it in the morning;
   I'd sing it in the evening
      all over this land;
   I'd sing out danger,
   I'd sing out a warning,
   I'd sing out love between my
      brothers and my sisters,
   All over this land.

4. Well, I got a hammer,
   And I've got a bell
   And I've got a song
      all over this land;
   It's the hammer of justice,
   It's the bell of freedom,
   It's the song about love
      between my brothers and my sisters,
   All over this land.

# IN MY ROOM

Words and Music by BRIAN WILSON
and GARY USHER

**Moderately slow**

There's a room where I can go and tell my se - crets to,
In this world I lock out all my wor - ries and my cares   in ____ my
Now it's dark and I'm a - lone but I won't be a - fraid,

room, ____ in ____ my room. ____
In my room.

room. ____ In my room. Do my dream - ing and my schem - ing,

lie a - wake and pray. ____ Do my cry - ing and my sigh - ing,

**D.C. al Coda**

laugh at yes - ter - day.

**CODA**

room. ____
In my room, in my

Room. ____
room, in my room, in my room, in my room.

# LITTLE GREEN APPLES

Words and Music by
BOBBY RUSSELL

**Slowly**

And I wake up in the morn - ing with my

hair down in my eyes and she says, "Hi." _____

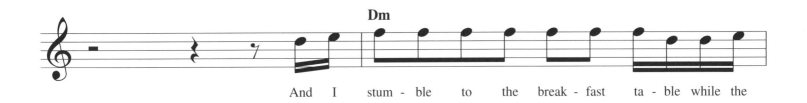

And I stum - ble to the break - fast ta - ble while the

kids are go - ing off to school, "Good - bye." _____

And she reach - es out an' takes my hand;
she drops what she's do - in' and

squeez - es it, says,"How you feel - in', Hon?"
hur - ries down to meet me and I'm al - ways late.

And I
But __

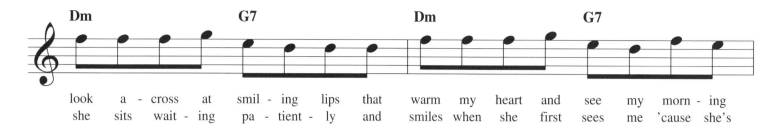

look a-cross at smil-ing lips that warm my heart and see my morn-ing
she sits wait-ing pa-tient-ly and smiles when she first sees me 'cause she's

sun.
made that way.

And if that's not lov-in' me,

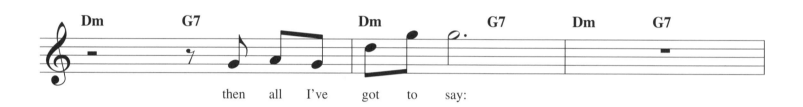

then all I've got to say:

God did-n't make lit-tle green ap-ples and it don't rain in In-dian-ap-'lis in the
God did-n't make lit-tle green ap-ples and it don't snow in Min-ne-ap-'lis when the

sum-mer-time. ___
win-ter comes. _

There's no such thing as Doc-tor Seuss,
There's no such thing as make-be-lieve,

Dis-ney-land, and Moth-er Goose is no nurs-'ry rhyme. ___
pup-py dogs and au-tumn leaves and ___ B. B. guns. ___

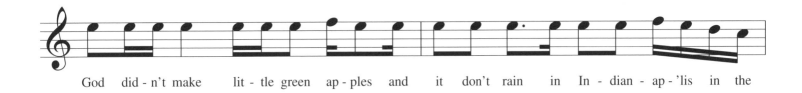

God did-n't make lit - tle green ap - ples and it don't rain in In - dian - ap - 'lis in the

sum-mer-time, ___ And when my - self is feel - in' low I

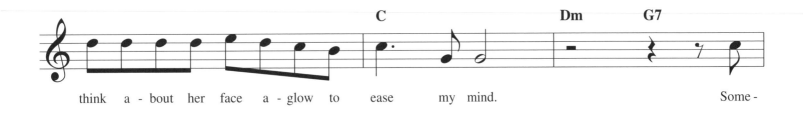

think a - bout her face a - glow to ease my mind. Some -

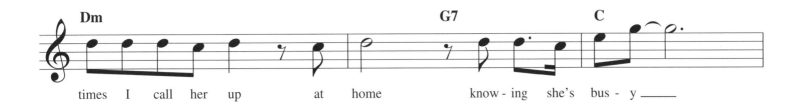

times I call her up at home know - ing she's bus - y _____

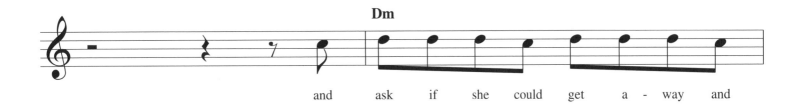

and ask if she could get a - way and

meet me _____ and grab a bite to eat. ___ And

# In the Midnight Hour

Words and Music by STEVE CROPPER
and WILSON PICKETT

**Moderately**

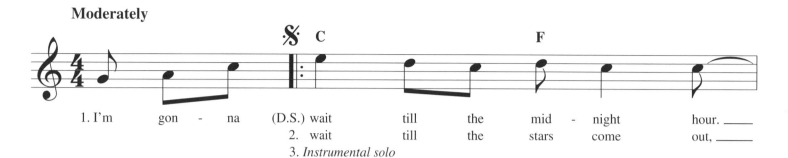

1. I'm gon - na (D.S.) wait till the mid - night hour. ____
2. wait till the stars come out, ____
3. *Instrumental solo*

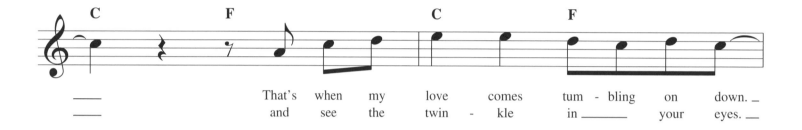

____ That's when my love comes tum - bling on down. _
____ and see the twin - kle in ____ your eyes. _

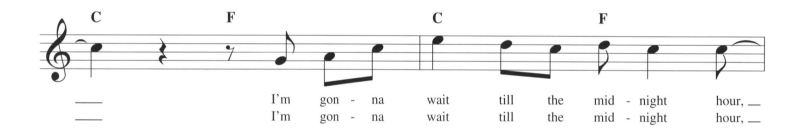

____ I'm gon - na wait till the mid - night hour, _
____ I'm gon - na wait till the mid - night hour, _

____ when there's no one else ____ a - round. _
____ that's where my love will be - gin to shine. _

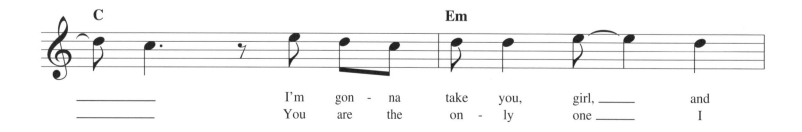

_____ I'm gon - na take you, girl, ____ and
_____ You are the on - ly one ____ I

# IT'S NOT UNUSUAL

Words and Music by GORDON MILLS
and LES REED

**With a strong beat**

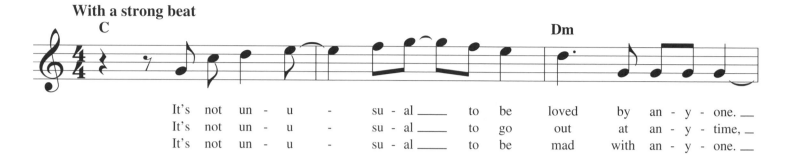

It's not un - u - su - al _____ to be loved by an - y - one. ___
It's not un - u - su - al _____ to go out at an - y - time, ___
It's not un - u - su - al _____ to be mad with an - y - one. ___

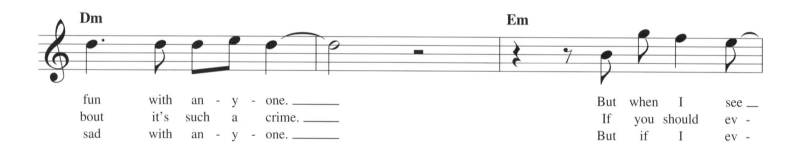

_____ It's not un - u - su - al _____ to have
_____ but when I see _____ you out ___ and a -
_____ It's not un - u - su - al _____ to be

fun with an - y - one. _____
bout it's such a crime. _____
sad with an - y - one. _____

But when I see _
If you should ev -
But if I ev -

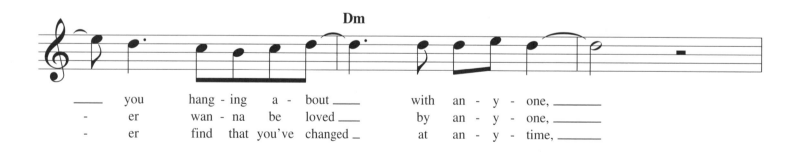

_____ you hang - ing a - bout _____ with an - y - one, _____
- er wan - na be loved ___ by an - y - one, _____
- er find that you've changed _ at an - y - time, _____

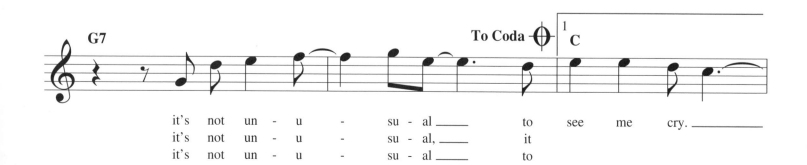

it's not un - u - su - al _____ to see me cry. _____
it's not un - u - su - al, _____ it
it's not un - u - su - al _____ to

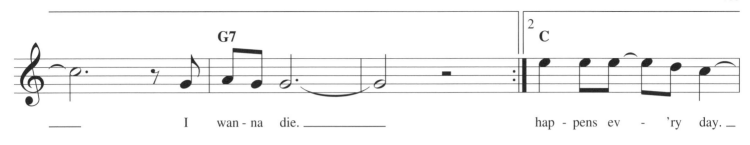

I wan - na die. _____ hap - pens ev - 'ry day. __

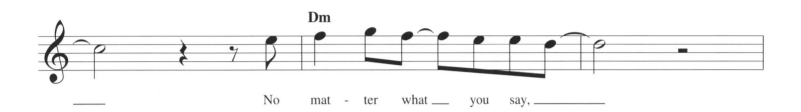

No mat - ter what __ you say, _____

you'll find it hap - pens all the time. _____

_____ Love will nev - er do

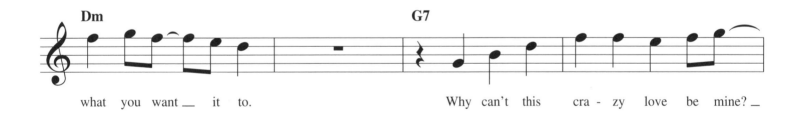

what you want __ it to. Why can't this cra - zy love be mine? __

**D.C. al Coda**

**CODA**

find that I'm __ in love __ with you. _____

# LEADER OF THE PACK

Words and Music by GEORGE MORTON,
JEFF BARRY and ELLIE GREENWICH

(Spoken:) *Is she really going out with him? There she is, let's ask her. Betty, is that Jimmy's ring you're wearing? (Mm-hm.) Gee, it must be great riding with him. Is he picking you up after school today? (Uh-uh.) By the way, where'd you meet him?*

I met him at the can - dy store, he turned a - round and smiled at me, you get the pic - ture? Yes, we see. That's when I fell for the lead - er of the pack.

My folks were al - ways put - ting him down.
One day my dad said find some - one new.
I felt so help - less, what could I do?

They said he came from the wrong side of town.
I had to tell my Jim - my we're through.
Re - mem - b'ring all the things we'd been through.

They told me he was bad, _____ but I know
He stood there and asked me why, _____ but all I could

he was sad, ____ that's why I fell for the lead-er of the
do was cry, ____ I'm sor-ry I hurt you, the lead-er of the

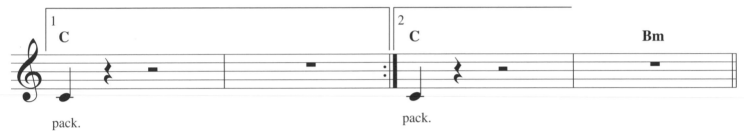

pack.

pack.

*(Spoken:) He sort of smiled and kissed me goodbye, but the tears were beginning to show as he drove away*

**D.S. al Coda**

*on that rainy night. I begged him to go slow, but whether he heard, I'll never know.*

**CODA**

In school they all stop and stare, ____ I can't hide the tears, but I don't care. __

I'll nev-er for-get ____ him, the lead-er of the pack.

# LEAVING ON A JET PLANE

Words and Music by
JOHN DENVER

# LET IT BE ME
## (Je T'appartiens)

English Words by MANN CURTIS
French Words by PIERRE DeLANOE
Music by GILBERT BECAUD

**Moderately**

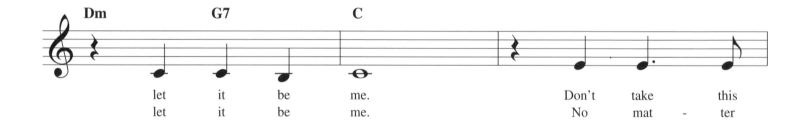

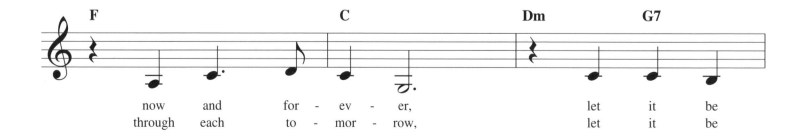

me.          Each     time     we     meet     love,

me.          To     you     I'm     pray - ing,

I     find     com - plete    love,          with - out     your

hear    what     I'm    say - ing,          please     let     your

sweet    love,          what    would    life     be?

heart    beat          for     me,     just     me.

So    nev - er    leave    me    lone - ly,        tell    me    you'll

And    nev - er    leave    me    lone - ly,        tell    me    you'll

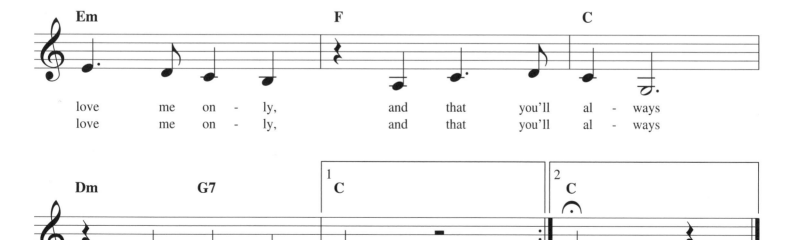

love    me    on - ly,        and    that    you'll    al - ways

love    me    on - ly,        and    that    you'll    al - ways

let    it    be    me.

let    it    be        me.

# LIGHTNIN' STRIKES

Words and Music by LOU CHRISTIE
and TWYLA HERBERT

# THE LOCO-MOTION

Words and Music by GERRY GOFFIN
and CAROLE KING

**Moderately**

Ev-'ry-bod-y's do - in' a brand - new dance_ now. (C'm on, ba - by, do _

_ the lo - co - mo - tion.) I know you'll get to like it if you give it a chance_ now.

(C'm on, ba - by, do _ the lo - co - mo - tion.) My lit - tle ba - by sis - ter can

do it with ease, _ it's eas - i - er than learn - in' your A - B - C's. _ So

come on, come on, do _ the lo - co - mo - tion with me. You got - ta

swing your hips now. Come on, ba - by, jump up, _ jump back. _

# LOUIE, LOUIE

Words and Music by
RICHARD BERRY

# MY GIRL

Words and Music by WILLIAM "SMOKEY" ROBINSON
and RONALD WHITE

**Moderately**

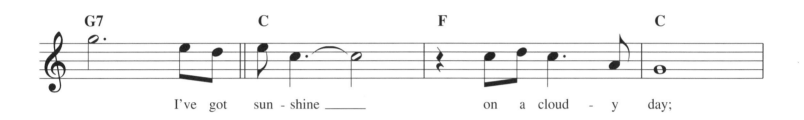

I've got sun - shine _____ on a cloud - y day;

when it's cold out - side, I've got the month of

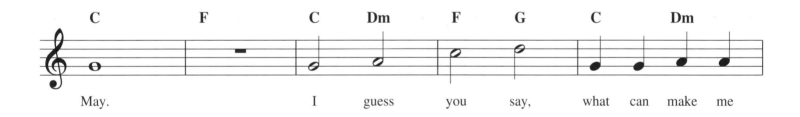

May. I guess you say, what can make me

feel this way? My girl, _____ talk - ing 'bout

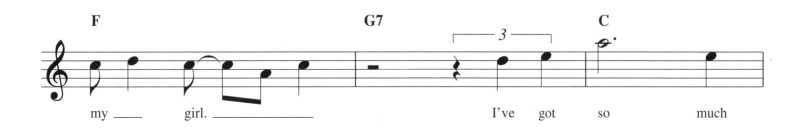

my ___ girl. _____ I've got so much

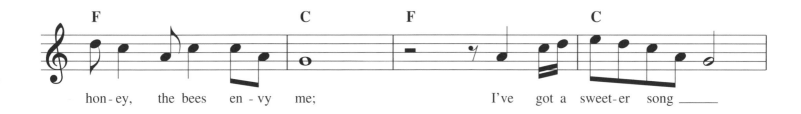

hon - ey, the bees en - vy me; I've got a sweet-er song _____

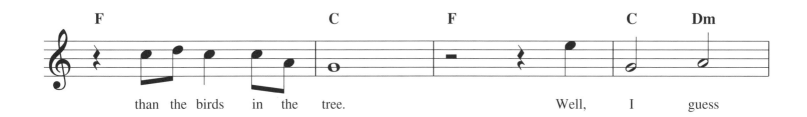

than the birds in the tree. Well, I guess

you say, what can make me feel this way? My girl, _____

_____ talk - ing 'bout my ___ girl. _____ I don't

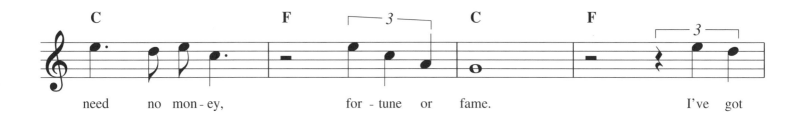

need no mon - ey, for - tune or fame. I've got

all the rich - es, ba - by, one man can claim. Well,

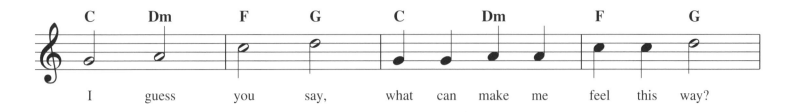

I guess you say, what can make me feel this way?

My girl, _____ talk -ing 'bout my ___ girl. _____

I've got sun -shine on a cloud - y day ___ with my girl; _____ I've

e - ven got the month of May with my girl. _____ Talk -ing 'bout, _

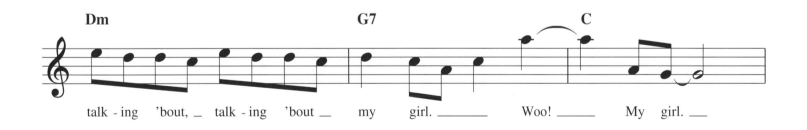

talk -ing 'bout, _ talk -ing 'bout _ my girl. _____ Woo! _____ My girl. _

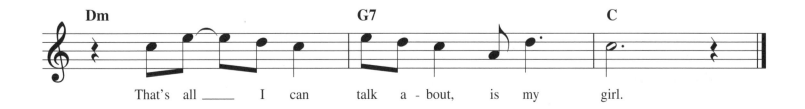

That's all _____ I can talk a -bout, is my girl.

# MAGIC CARPET RIDE

Words and Music by JOHN KAY
and RUSHTON MOREVE

**Heavy Metal Rock**

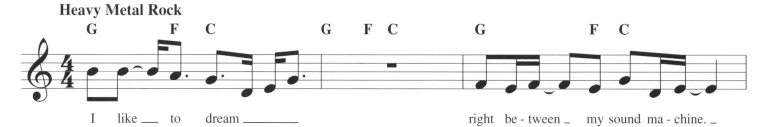

I like to dream right be-tween my sound ma-chine.

On a cloud of sound I drift in the night,

an-y place it goes is right; goes far, flies near,

to the stars a-way from here. Well, you don't know what

we can find. Oh, why don't you come with me, lit-tle girl,

on a mag-ic car-pet ride. Well, you don't know what

we can see.        Why don't you tell your dreams to me,

fan - tas - y ____ will set you free.        Close your eyes, girl,        look in - side, girl,

let    the sound take you a - way.        Last

night I owned ____ A - lad - din's lamp ____        and so I wished that I could stay.

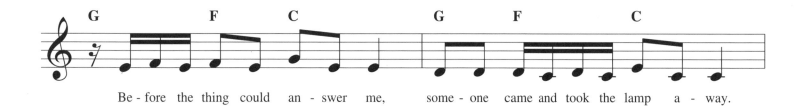

Be - fore the thing could an - swer me,        some - one came and took the lamp a - way.

**D.S. and Fade**

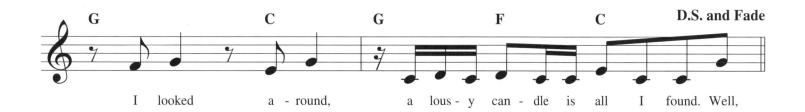

I looked       a - round,        a lous - y can - dle is all I found. Well,

# MARY IN THE MORNING

Words and Music by JOHNNY CYMBAL
and MIKE LENDELL

**Sweetly**

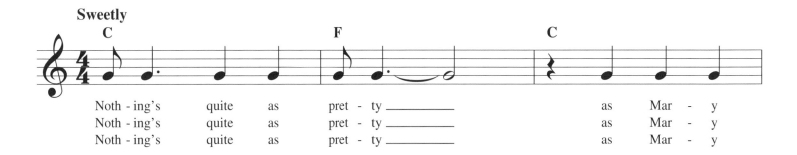

Noth - ing's quite as pret - ty _____ as Mar - y
Noth - ing's quite as pret - ty _____ as Mar - y
Noth - ing's quite as pret - ty _____ as Mar - y

in the morn - ing, when through a sleep - y haze ___ I
in the morn - ing, chas - ing a rain - bow in ___ her
in the morn - ing, kissed by the shades of night ___ and

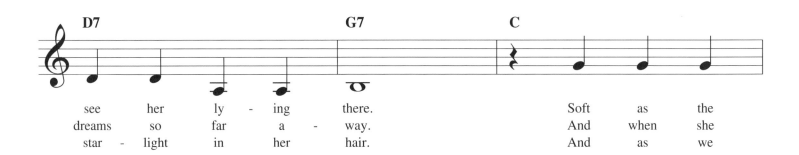

see her ly - ing there. Soft as the
dreams so far a - way. And when she
star - light in her hair. And as we

rain that falls on sum - mer flow - ers
turns to touch it I kiss her face so soft - ly,
walk I hold her close be - side me;

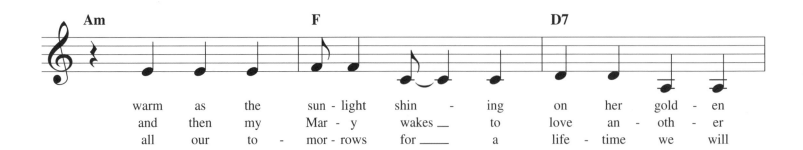

warm as the sun - light shin - ing on her gold - en
and then my Mar - y wakes ___ to love an - oth - er
all our to - mor - rows for ___ a life - time we will

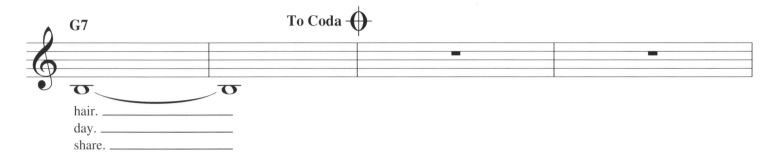

hair. _____

day. _____

share. _____

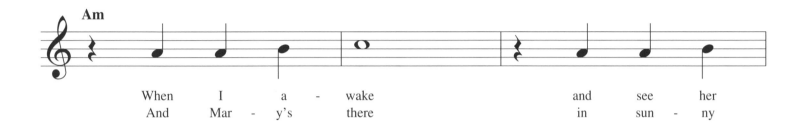

When I a - wake     and see her

And Mar - y's there     in sun - ny

there so close be - side me. _____ I want to

days or storm - y weath - er. _____ She does - n't

take     her in my arms; the ache is

care     'cause right or wrong, the love we

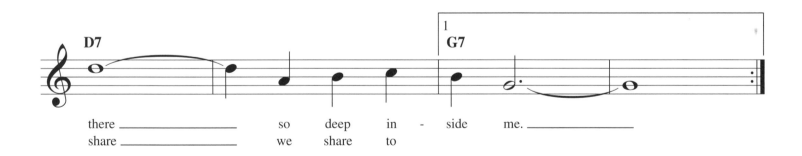

there _____ so deep in - side me. _____

share _____ we share to

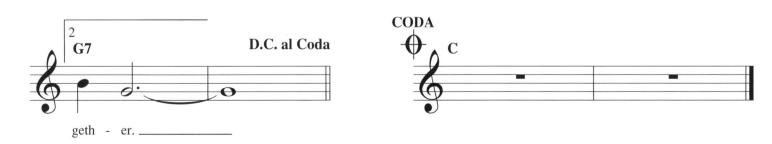

geth - er. _____

# MIDNIGHT CONFESSIONS

Words and Music by
LOU JOSIE

you wear on your hand _____ makes me un -

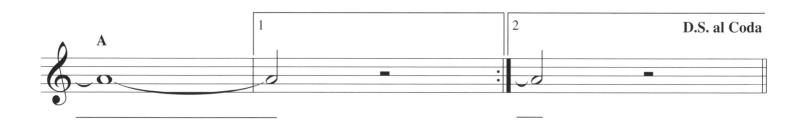

- der - stand, _____ there's an - oth - er be - fore ___

_____ me. You'll nev - er be mine. _____ I'm wast - ing my time. _

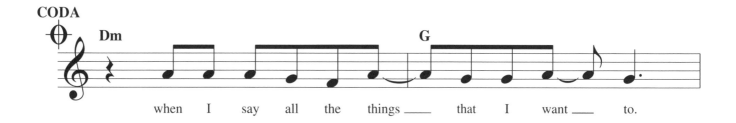

when I say all the things ___ that I want ___ to.

La la la la _____ la la la ___ la. La la la la ___

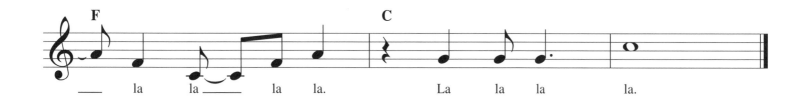

_____ la la ___ la la. La la la la.

# MONDAY, MONDAY

Words and Music by
JOHN PHILLIPS

**Steady Rock**

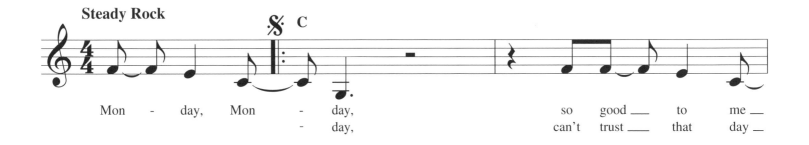

Mon - day, Mon - day,      so good ___ to me ___
- day,      can't trust ___ that day ___

Mon - day morn - in', it ___ was all ___
Mon - day, Mon - day, some - times it

___ I hoped it would be. _____      Oh, Mon - day
just turns out ___ that way. _____      Oh, Mon - day

morn - in', Mon - day morn - in' could - n't guar - an - tee, ___
morn - in', you gave me no warn - in' of what was to be, ___

that Mon - day eve - nin' you would still be here ___ with
oh, Mon - day, Mon - day, how could you still leave and not ___ take

me.                                                                 Mon - day, Mon - me?

Ev - 'ry oth - er day, _____ ev - 'ry

oth - er day, ev - 'ry oth - er day of the week is fine,

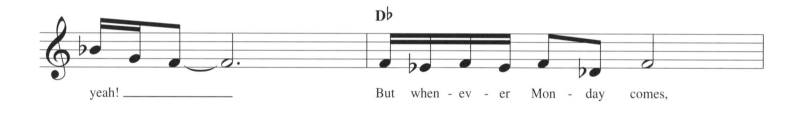

yeah! _____ But when - ev - er Mon - day comes,

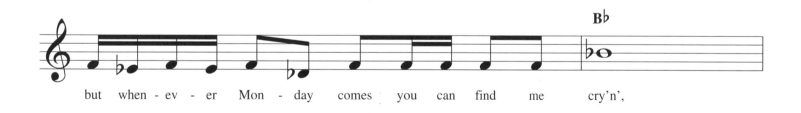

but when - ev - er Mon - day comes you can find me cry'n',

yeah! _____ Mon - day, Mon -

# MOON RIVER

**from the Paramount Picture BREAKFAST AT TIFFANY'S**

Words by JOHNNY MERCER
Music by HENRY MANCINI

**Slow Waltz**

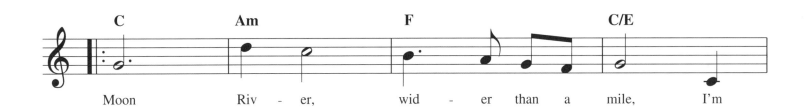

Moon Riv - er, wid - er than a mile, I'm

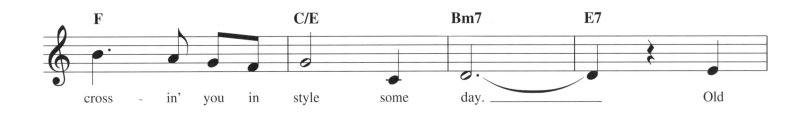

cross - in' you in style some day. _____ Old

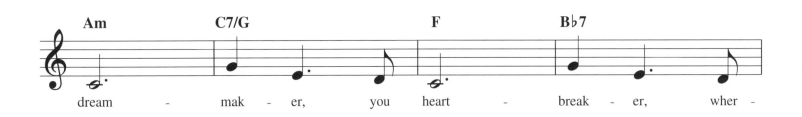

dream - mak - er, you heart - break - er, wher -

ev - er you're go - in', ____ I'm go - in' ____ your way.

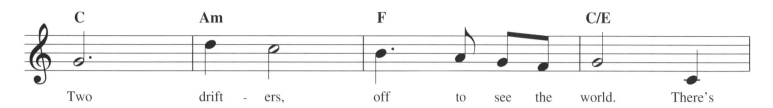

Two    drift - ers,    off   to   see   the   world.    There's

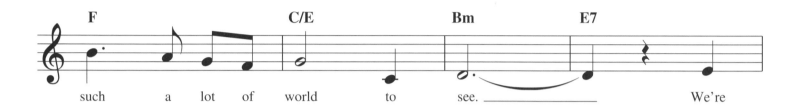

such   a   lot   of   world   to   see. _____   We're

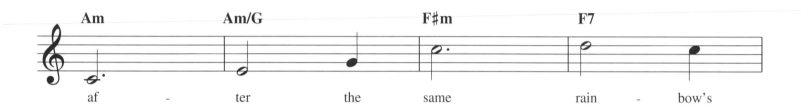

af - ter   the   same   rain - bow's

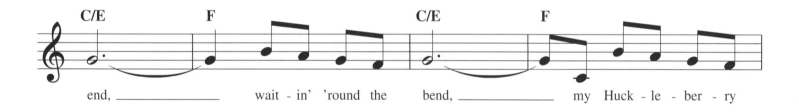

end, _____   wait - in' 'round the   bend, _____   my Huck - le - ber - ry

friend,   Moon   Riv - er _____   and

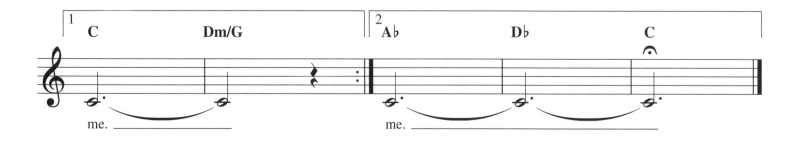

me. _____         me. _____

# MY BOYFRIEND'S BACK

Words and Music by ROBERT FELDMAN,
GERALD GOLDSTEIN and RICHARD GOTTEHRER

# MY LOVE

Words and Music by
TONY HATCH

**Moderately**

My love is warm-er than the warm-est ____ sun - shine,

soft - er than a sigh. ____ My love is deep-er than the

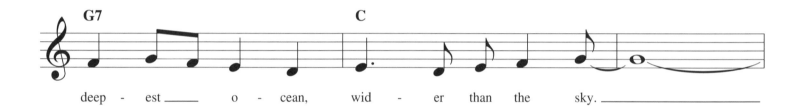

deep - est ____ o - cean, wid - er than the sky. ____

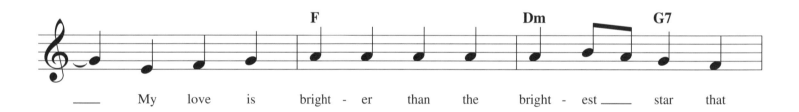

____ My love is bright - er than the bright - est ____ star that

shines ev - 'ry night a - bove ____ and there is noth - ing in this

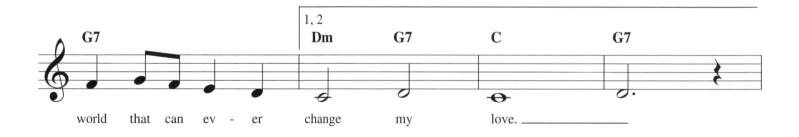

world that can ev - er change my love. ____

# ONLY THE LONELY
## (Know the Way I Feel)

Words and Music by ROY ORBISON
and JOE MELSON

# SAN FRANCISCO
## (Be Sure to Wear Some Flowers in Your Hair)

Words and Music by
JOHN PHILLIPS

**Gently**

If you're go-ing __ to San Fran - cis - co, __

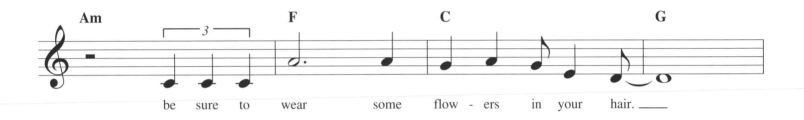

be sure to wear some flow-ers in your hair. __

If you're __ go - in' __ to San Fran - cis - co, __

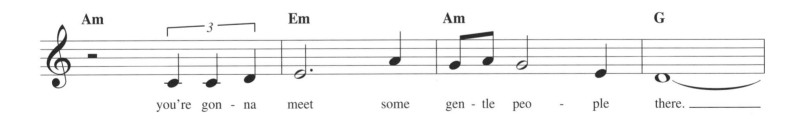

you're gon - na meet some gen - tle peo - ple there. __

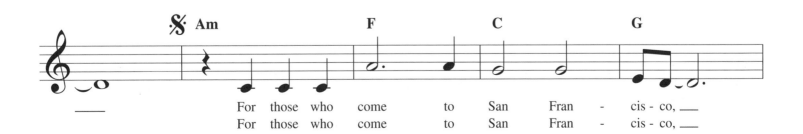

For those who come to San Fran - cis - co, __
For those who come to San Fran - cis - co, __

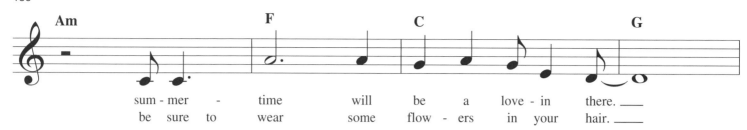

sum - mer - time will be a love - in there. ___
be sure to wear some flow - ers in your hair. ___

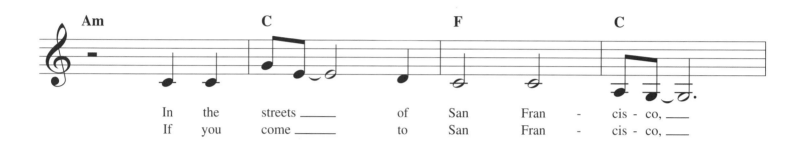

In the streets ___ of San Fran - cis - co, ___
If you come ___ to San Fran - cis - co, ___

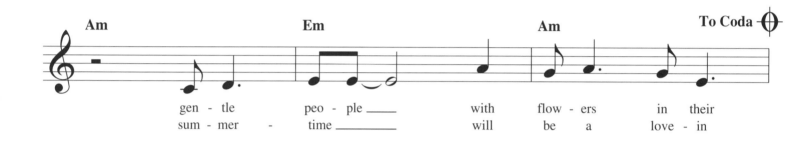

**To Coda**

gen - tle peo - ple ___ with flow - ers in their
sum - mer - time ___ will be a love - in

hair. ___ All a - cross the na - tion, ___

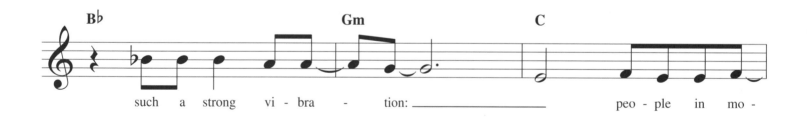

such a strong vi - bra - tion: ___ peo - ple in mo -

- tion. ___ There's a whole gen - er - a - tion ___

with a new ex - pla - na - tion. _____ Peo - ple in mo -

D.S. al Coda

- tion. ___ Peo - ple in mo - tion. ___

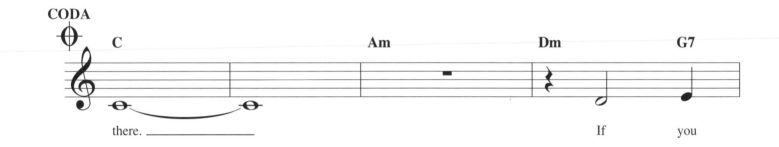

CODA

there. _____ If you

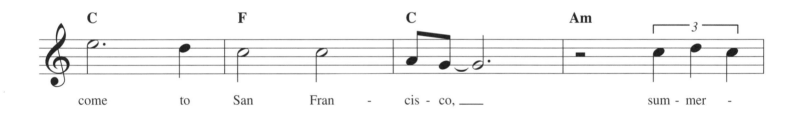

come to San Fran - cis - co, ___ sum - mer -

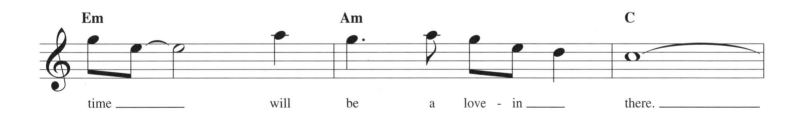

time _____ will be a love - in ___ there. _____

# PUPPY LOVE

Words and Music by
PAUL ANKA

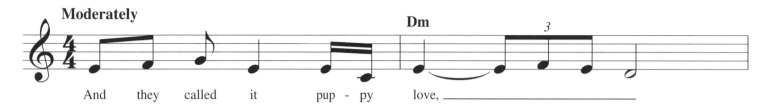

And they called it pup - py love, _____

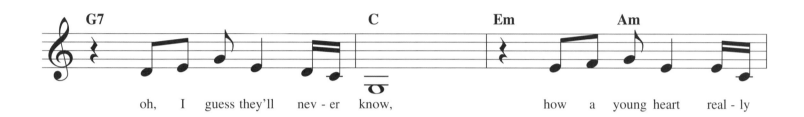

oh, I guess they'll nev - er know,          how a young heart real - ly

feels, _____          and ___ why I love her

so. ___          And they called it pup - py love _____

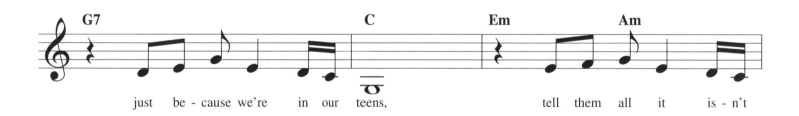

just be - cause we're in our teens,          tell them all it is - n't

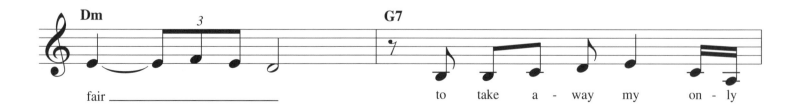

fair _____          to take a - way my on - ly

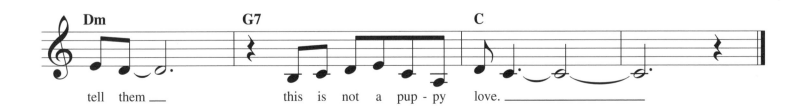

# RELEASE ME

Words and Music by ROBERT YOUNT,
EDDIE MILLER and DUB WILLIAMS

**Slow Country**

Please re - lease me, let me go, _____ for
I have found a new love, dear, _____ and

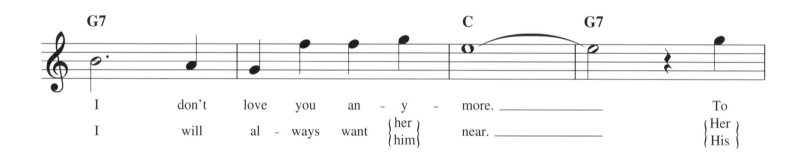

I don't love you an - y - more. _____ To
I will al - ways want {her}{him} near. _____ {Her}{His}

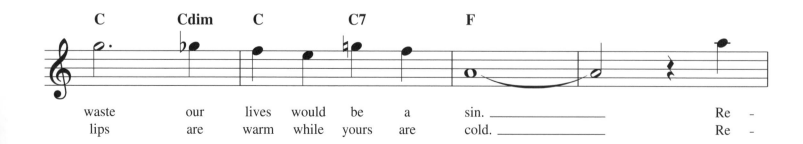

waste our lives would be a sin. _____ Re -
lips are warm while yours are cold. _____ Re -

lease me, and let me love a - gain.
lease me, my dar - ling, let me

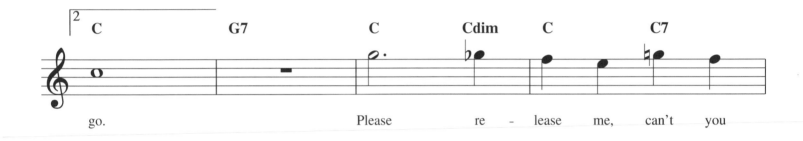

go. Please re - lease me, can't you

see _____ you'd be a fool to cling to me. _____

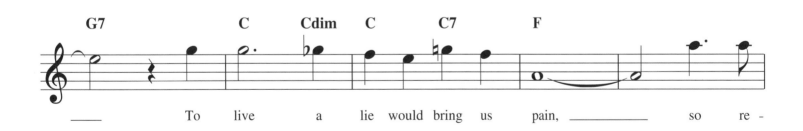

_____ To live a lie would bring us pain, _____ so re -

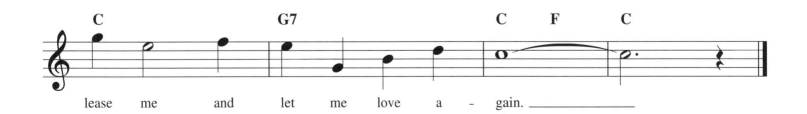

lease me and let me love a - gain. _____

# RESPECT

Words and Music by
OTIS REDDING

**Moderate Rock**

What you want ba - by I got.
I ain't gon - na do you wrong while you gone.

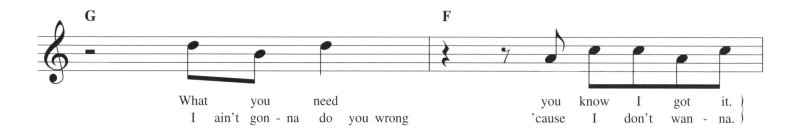

What you need you know I got it. }
I ain't gon - na do you wrong 'cause I don't wan - na. }

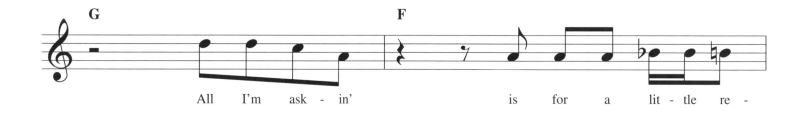

All I'm ask - in' is for a lit - tle re -

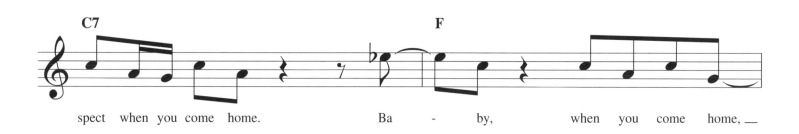

spect when you come home. Ba - by, when you come home, ___

___ re - spect.
I'm out ___ to give you
Ooh, ___ your kiss - es,

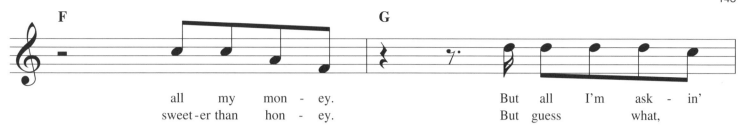

all my mon - ey. But all I'm ask - in'
sweet - er than hon - ey. But guess what,

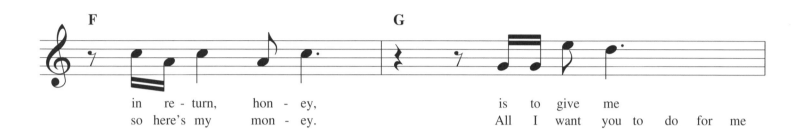

in re - turn, hon - ey, is to give me
so here's my mon - ey. All I want you to do for me

my pro - per re - spect }
is give me some here } when you get home. Yeah, ba - by, when you get

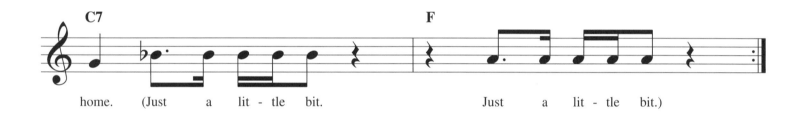

home. (Just a lit - tle bit. Just a lit - tle bit.)

R - E - S - P - E - C - T, find out what it means to me,

R - E - S - P - E - C - T, take out T - C - P.

**Repeat and Fade**

A lit - tle re - spect.

# RUBY BABY

Words and Music by JERRY LEIBER
and MIKE STOLLER

**Moderately**

I love a girl and-a Ru-by is her name. ___
Each time I see you, ___ ba-by, my heart cries. ___

This girl don't __ love me but I love her just the same. ___
Tell yuh, I'm gon-na steal __ you a - way from all those guys. ___

Ru-by, Ru-by, how I want yuh, like a ghost I'm a
From the hap-py day I met yuh, I made a bet that I was

gon - na haunt yuh. Ru - by, Ru - by, Ru - by, will you be
gon - na get yuh. Ru - by, Ru - by, Ru - by, will you be

mine?
mine? Ru - by, Ru - by, Ru - by, ba - by.

Ru - by, Ru - by, Ru - by, ba - by. Ru - by, Ru - by,

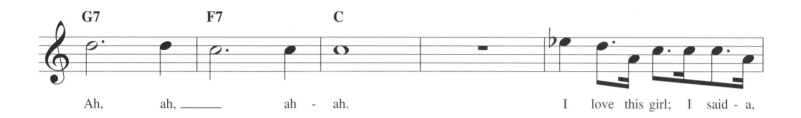

Ru - by, ba - by. Ru - by, Ru - by, Ru - by, ba - by.

Ah, ah, _____ ah - ah. I love this girl; I said - a,

Ru - by is her name. __ When this girl looks at me she just

sets my heart a - flame. __ Got some hug - gin' and

kiss - es too, yeah, and I'm gon - na give them - a all to you. Now lis - ten,

Ru - by, Ru - by, when will you be mine?

Ru - by, Ru - by, when will you be mine? _____

# SAVE THE LAST DANCE FOR ME

Words and Music by DOC POMUS
and MORT SHUMAN

**Moderately**

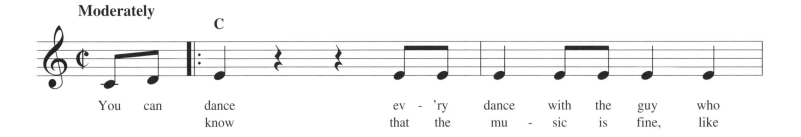

You can dance ev - 'ry dance with the guy who
know that the mu - sic is fine, like

gave you the eye; let him hold you tight. ___
spar - kling wine; ___ go and have your fun. ___

You can smile ev - 'ry smile for the man who
Laugh and sing but while we're a - part ___ don't

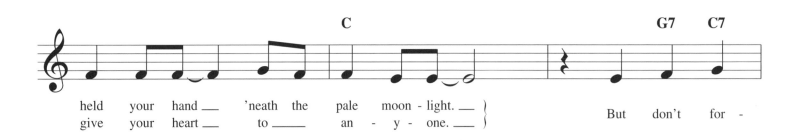

held your hand ___ 'neath the pale moon - light. ___ )
give your heart ___ to ___ an - y - one. ___ )

But don't for -

get who's tak - ing you home and in whose arms you're

gon - na be. ____ So dar - lin' _____ save the

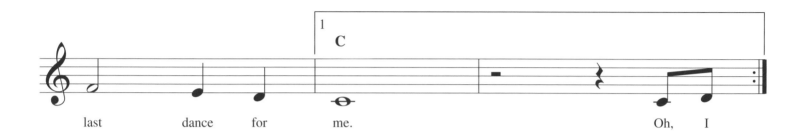

last dance for me. Oh, I

me. Ba - by, don't you know I love you so? _____

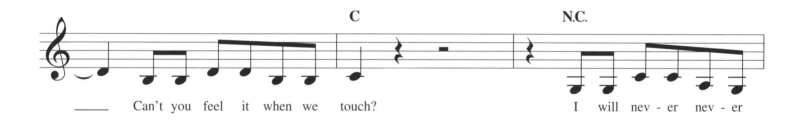

____ Can't you feel it when we touch? I will nev - er nev - er

let you go. ____ I love you, oh, so much.

You can dance, go and car - ry on ____ till the

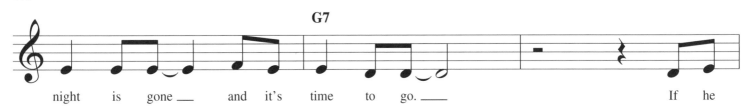

**G7**

night is gone ___ and it's time to go. ___ If he

asks if you're all a - lone, ___ can he

**C**

take you home, ___ you must tell him no. ___

**G7**   **C**   **F**

'Cause don't for - get who's tak - ing you home and in whose arms you're

**C**                                    **G7**

gon - na be. ___ So, dar - lin' ___ save the

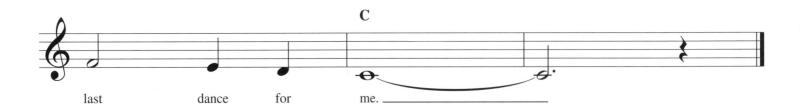

**C**

last dance for me. ___

# SOMEBODY TO LOVE

Words and Music by
DARBY SLICK

**Moderately fast**

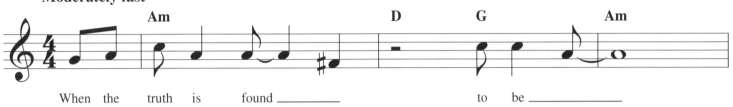

When the truth is found _____ to be _____

lies, and all of the joy _____ with - in you _____

___ dies, don't you want some - bod - y to love? _

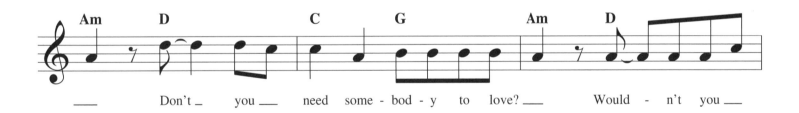

___ Don't _ you _ need some - bod - y to love? ___ Would - n't you ___

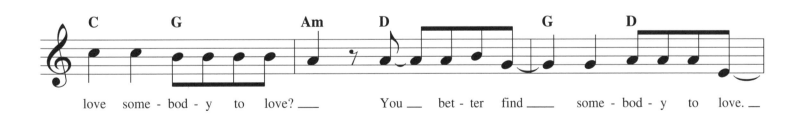

love some - bod - y to love? ___ You _ bet - ter find _____ some - bod - y to love. _

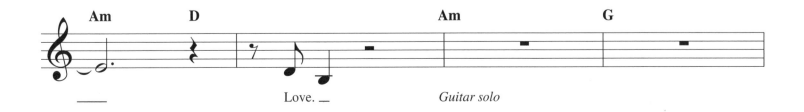

___ Love. _ *Guitar solo*

# (SITTIN' ON) THE DOCK OF THE BAY

Words and Music by STEVE CROPPER
and OTIS REDDING

153

# SO NICE
## (Summer Samba)

Original Words and Music by MARCOS VALLE
and PAULO SERGIO VALLE
English Words by NORMAN GIMBEL

**Moderately**

Some - one to hold me tight, that would be ver - y nice,

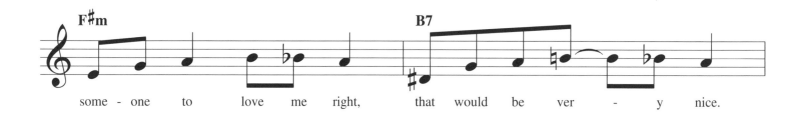

some - one to love me right, that would be ver - y nice.

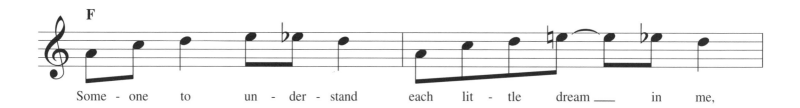

Some - one to un - der - stand each lit - tle dream ___ in me,

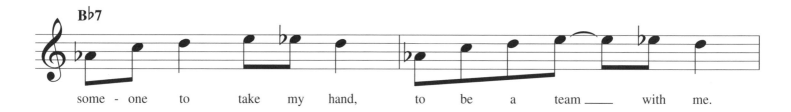

some - one to take my hand, to be a team ___ with me.

So nice, _____ life would be so nice _____

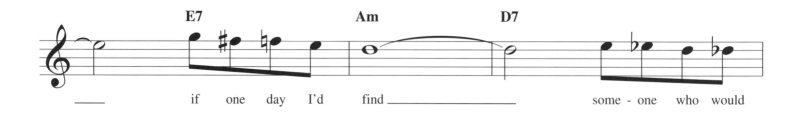

___ if one day I'd find _____ some - one who would

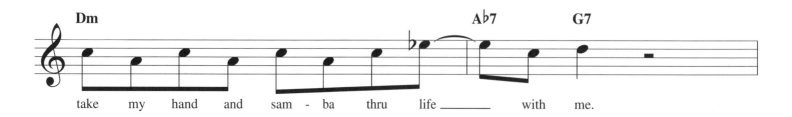

take my hand and sam - ba thru life _____ with me.

Some - one  to  cling  to  me,  stay  with  me  right ____ or  wrong,

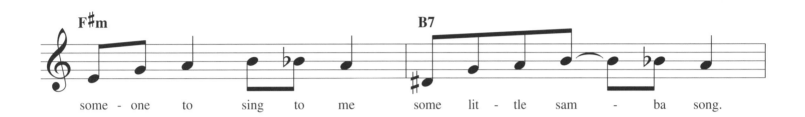

some - one  to  sing  to  me  some  lit - tle  sam - ba  song.

Some - one  to  take  my  heart,  then  give  his  heart ____ to  me.

Some - one  who's  read - y  to  give  love  a  start ____ with  me.

Oh,  yes, _____ that  would  be  so  nice. _____

____ Should  it  be  you  and  me,  I  could  see  it  would  be

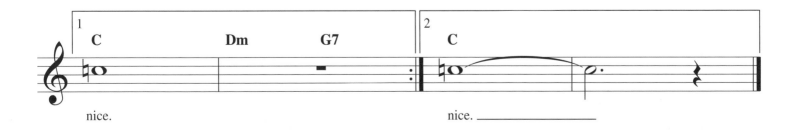

nice.  nice. _____

# SOMETHING

Words and Music by
GEORGE HARRISON

**Moderately**

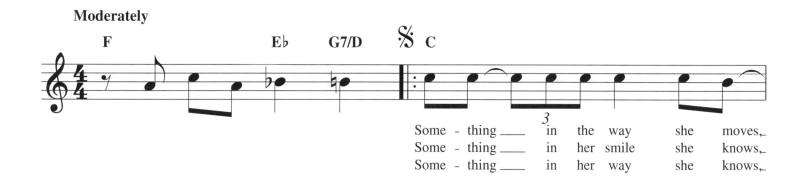

Some - thing \_\_\_\_ in the way she moves,
Some - thing \_\_\_\_ in her smile she knows,
Some - thing \_\_\_\_ in her way she knows,

_____ at - tracts me like no oth - er lov - er.
_____ that I don't need no oth - er lov - er.
_____ and all I have to do is think of her.

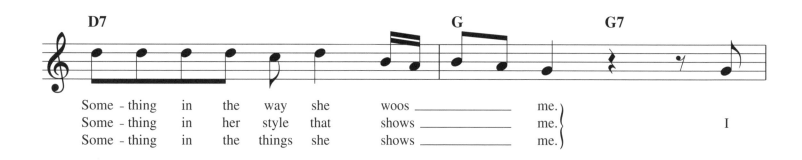

Some - thing in the way she woos _____ me.
Some - thing in her style that shows _____ me.
Some - thing in the things she shows _____ me.

I

**To Coda**

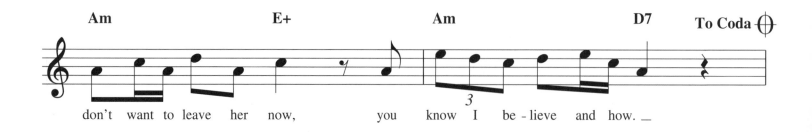

don't want to leave her now, you know I be - lieve and how. \_\_

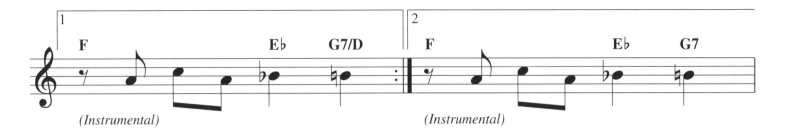

(Instrumental)                    (Instrumental)

You're ask - ing  me  will  my love  grow,     I  don't

know, ___ I ___ don't know.     You stick a - round now,  it may

show,     I  don't  know, ___ I ___ don't know.

**D.S. al Coda**

**CODA**

(Instrumental)

# SOUL MAN

Words and Music by ISAAC HAYES
and DAVID PORTER

**Moderately**

Com - in' to ya' on a dust - y road;
what I got the hard way, and I'll
brought up on a side street. I

good ___ lov - in', I got a truck load. ___ And
make it bet - ter each and ev - 'ry ___ day.
learned how to love be - fore I could ___ eat. I was

when you get it, you got some. ___ So,
So, hon - ey, don't you fret, 'cause
ed - u - cat - ed at Wood - stock. ___ When

don't ___ wor - ry, 'cause I'm com - in'.
you ___ ain't ___ seen noth - ing ___ yet. I'm a
I ___ start lov - in', oh, I can't ___ stop.

soul man, ___ (Instrumental) I'm a soul man. ___ (Instrumental)

I'm a soul man, — *(Instrumental)* I'm a

soul man. — *(Instrumental)* Got *(Instrumental)* I was

Grab the rope — and I'll pull you in, ___ give you hope, and

be your on - ly boy - friend, yeah, — yeah, — yeah, — yeah. *(Instrumental)*

Talk - in' a - bout a

soul man, ___ I'm a soul man. ___ Soul ___ man; ___

soul man; — I'm a soul man; — I'm a soul man. _____

# SPANISH EYES

Words by CHARLES SINGLETON and EDDIE SNYDER
Music by BERT KAEMPFERT

**Moderately**

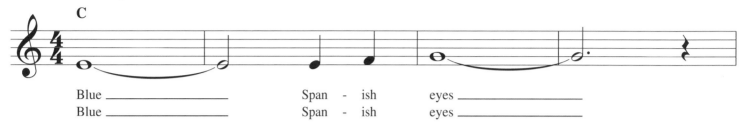

Blue _____ Span - ish eyes _____
Blue _____ Span - ish eyes _____

tear - drops are fall - ing from your Span - ish eyes. _____
pret - ti - est eyes in all of Mex - i - co. _____

Please, _____ please don't cry _____
True _____ Span - ish eyes _____

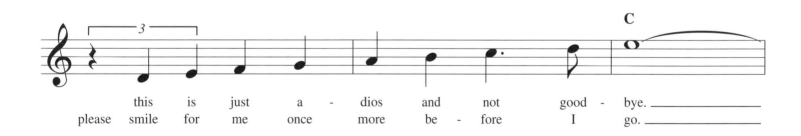

this is just a - dios and not good - bye. _____
please smile for me once more be - fore I go. _____

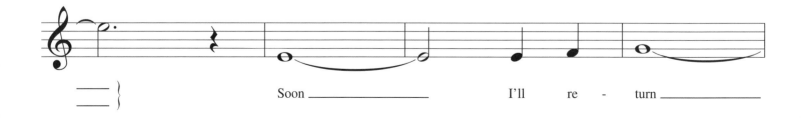

___ Soon _____ I'll re - turn _____

bring - ing   you   all   the   love   your   heart   can

hold. _____          Please _____        say    si

si, _____          say    you    and    your   Span - ish

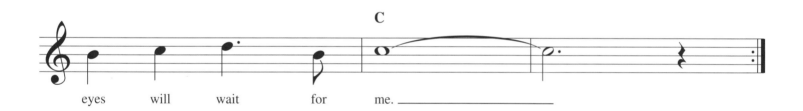

eyes    will    wait    for    me. _____

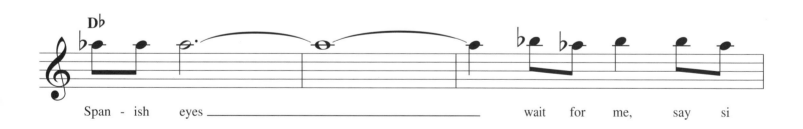

Span - ish   eyes _____        wait   for   me,   say   si

si! _____

# STAY

Words and Music by
MAURICE WILLIAMS

**Moderately**

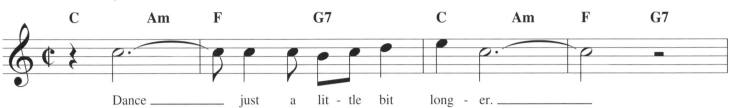

Dance _____ just a lit - tle bit long - er. _____

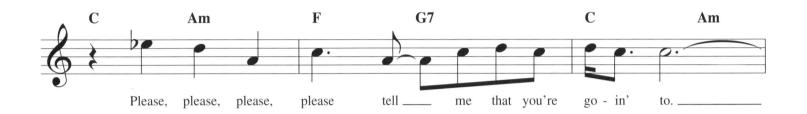

Please, please, please, please tell _____ me that you're go - in' to. _____

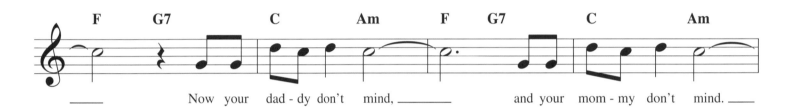

_____ Now your dad - dy don't mind, _____ and your mom - my don't mind. _____

_____ Could we have an - oth - er dance, dear? _____ Just - a one more,

one _____ more _____ time. Oh, won't you stay _____

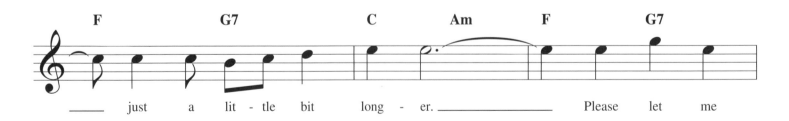

_____ just a lit - tle bit long - er. _____ Please let me

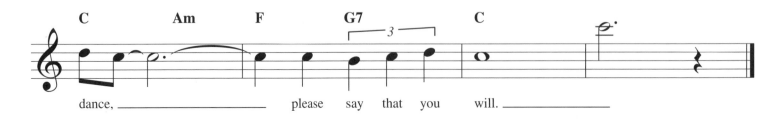

dance, _____ please say that you will. _____

# SWEET CAROLINE

Words and Music by
NEIL DIAMOND

Moderately, very steady

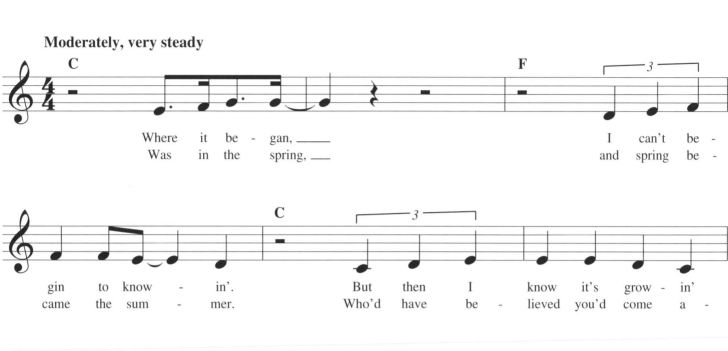

Where it be - gan, _____ I can't be -
Was in the spring, _____ and spring be -

gin to know - in'. But then I know it's grow - in'
came the sum - mer. Who'd have be - lieved you'd come a -

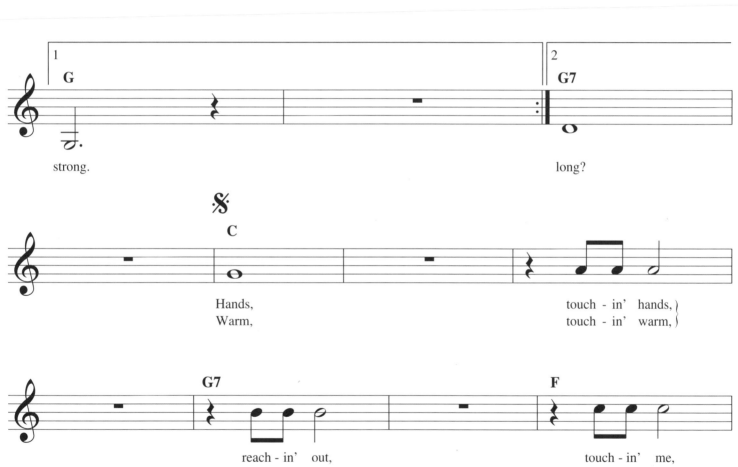

strong.

long?

Hands,
Warm,

touch - in' hands,
touch - in' warm,

reach - in' out,

touch - in' me,

touch - in' you. _____

Sweet Car - o - line, _____

**CODA**

*(Instrumental)*

Sweet    Car - o - line, ____

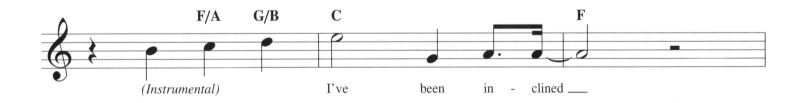

good    times    nev - er    seemed    so    good.

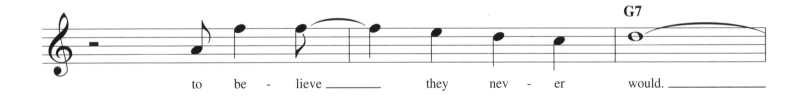

*(Instrumental)*    I've    been    in - clined ____

good.    to    be - lieve ____    they    nev - er    would. ____

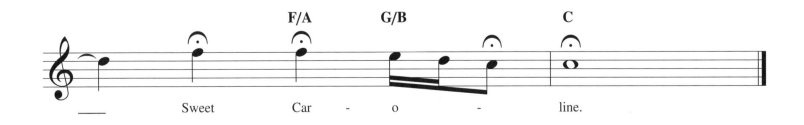

____    Sweet    Car - o - line.

# STORMY

Words and Music by J.R. COBB
and BUDDY BUIE

**Moderately**

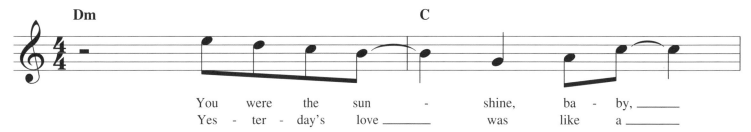

You were the sun - shine, ba - by, _____
Yes - ter - day's love _____ was like a _____

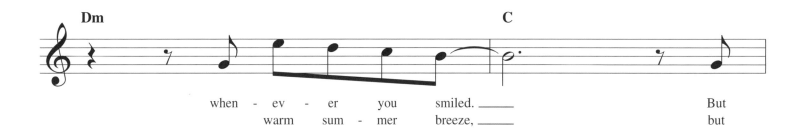

when - ev - er you smiled. _____ But
warm sum - mer breeze, _____ but

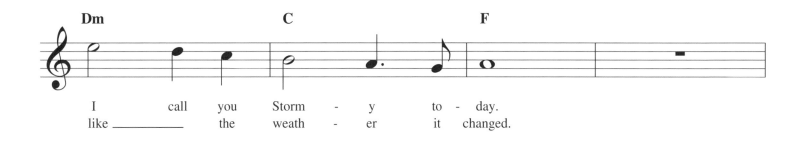

I call you Storm - y to - day.
like _____ the weath - er it changed.

All of a sud - den that old _____ rain's fall - in' down _____
Now things are drear - y, ba - by, and it's wind - y and cold _____
*Instrumental*

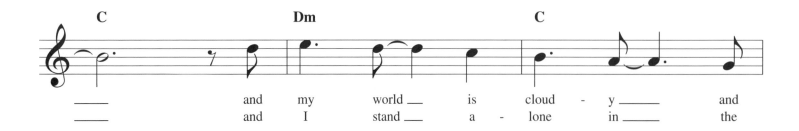

_____ and my world _____ is cloud - y _____ and
_____ and I stand _____ a - lone in _____ the

# STRANGERS IN THE NIGHT
**Adapted from A MAN COULD GET KILLED**

Words by CHARLES SINGLETON and EDDIE SNYDER
Music by BERT KAEMPFERT

**Moderately slow**

Stran - gers in the night _____ ex - chang - ing glanc - es,

won - d'ring in the night _____ what were the chanc - es

we'd be shar - ing love _____ be - fore the night was

through. _____ Some - thing in your eyes _____

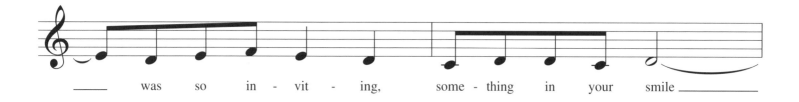

_____ was so in - vit - ing, some - thing in your smile _____

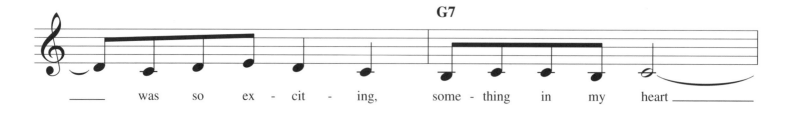

_____ was so ex - cit - ing, some - thing in my heart _____

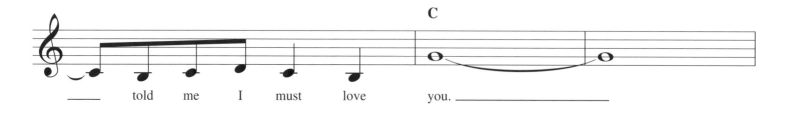

_____ told me I must love you. _____

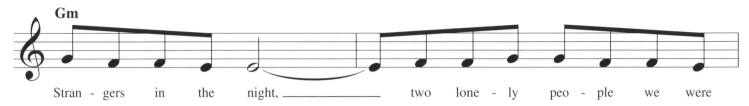

Gm

Stran - gers in the night, _____ two lone - ly peo - ple we were

A7

stran - gers in the night _____ up to the mo - ment when we

Dm                                          Fm

said our first hel - lo,                    lit - tle did we know

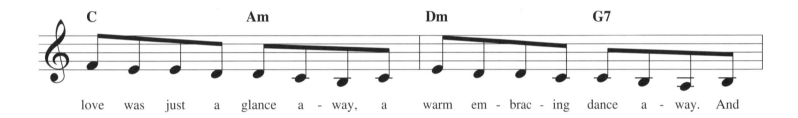

C                    Am              Dm                    G7

love was just a glance a - way, a warm em - brac - ing dance a - way. And

C

ev - er since that night _____ we've been to - geth - er,

lov - ers at first sight _____ in love for - ev - er,

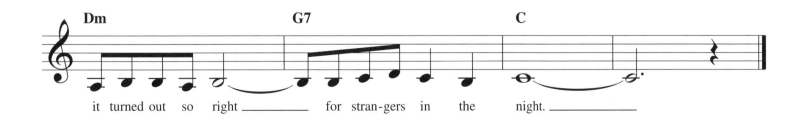

Dm                    G7                    C

it turned out so right _____ for stran - gers in the night. _____

# SURF CITY

Words and Music by BRIAN WILSON
and JAN BERRY

**Moderately**

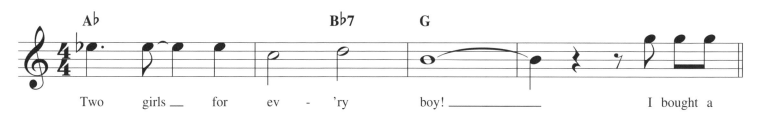

Two girls ___ for ev - 'ry boy! _____ I bought a

thir - ty - four wag - on and we call it a wood - y.
nev - er roll the streets up 'cause there's al - ways some - thing go - ing.
wood - y breaks down on me some - where on my surf ___ route,

Surf Cit - y, here we come! { You know it's
{ They're ___
{ I'll strap my

not ver - y cher - ry as an old - ie, but a good - ie.
ei - ther out surf - in' or they got a par - ty go - in'.
board to my back and hitch a ride in my wet suit.

Surf Cit - y, here we come! { Well, it ain't got a back seat or a
{ There's ___ two swing - in' hon - eys for ___
{ When I get to Surf Cit - y I'll be

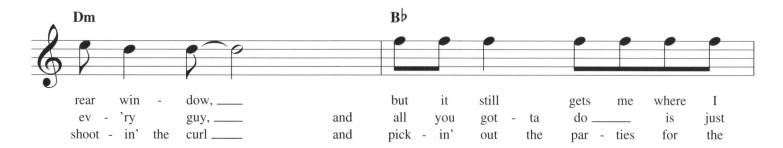

rear win - dow, ___ but it still gets me where I
ev - 'ry guy, ___ and all you got - ta do _____ is just
shoot - in' the curl ___ and pick - in' out the par - ties for the

# TAKE A LETTER, MARIA

Words and Music by
R.B. GREAVES

**Moderately**

1. Last _____ night as I got _____ home a - bout _____ a half - past ten, _____
2., 3. *(See additional lyrics)*

_____ there _____ was the wom - an I thought _____ I knew in the

arms of an - oth - er man. _____ I kept _____ my cool, _____ I ain't _____

_____ no fool, _____ let me tell you what hap - pened then, _____ I packed _____

_____ some clothes _____ and I _____ walked out, _____ and I ain't goin' back a - gain. _____

**Chorus**

_____ So take a let - ter, Ma - ri - a, ad -

dress it to my wife.  Say I won't be com - ing home, ___

___ got - ta start a new life.  So take a

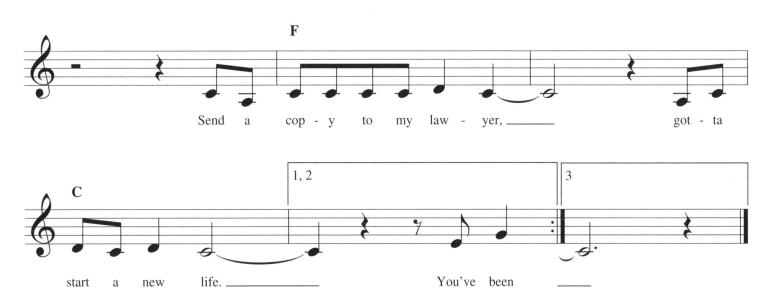

let - ter, Ma - ri - a,  ad - dress it to my wife.

Send a cop - y to my law - yer, _____ got - ta

**1, 2**

**3**

start a new life. _____ You've been _____

*Additional Lyrics*

2. You've been many things, but most of all a good secretary to me,
And it's times like this I feel you've always been close to me.
Was I wrong to work nights to try to build a good life?
All work and no play has just cost me a wife.
*(Chorus)*

3. When a man loves a woman, it's hard to understand
That she would find more pleasure in the arms of another man.
I never really noticed how sweet you are to me,
It just so happens I'm free tonight, would you like to have dinner with me?
*(Chorus)*

# THIS IS MY SONG
### from Charles Chaplin's A COUNTESS FROM HONG KONG - A Universal Release

Words and Music by
CHARLES CHAPLIN

**Romantically**

Why is my heart so light? Why are the stars so
Flow-ers are smil-ing bright. Smi-ling for our de-

bright? Why is the sky so blue _____ since the
light. Smil-ing so ten-der-ly _____ for the

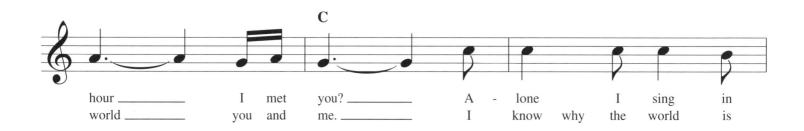

hour _____ I met you? _____ A-lone I sing in
world _____ you and me. _____ I know why the world is

moon-light _____ with you in my heart su-preme. _____ To
smil-ing, _____ smil-ing so ten-der-ly; _____ it

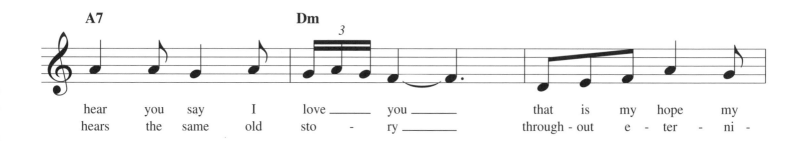

hear you say I love _____ you _____ that is my hope my
hears the same old sto-ry _____ through-out e-ter-ni-

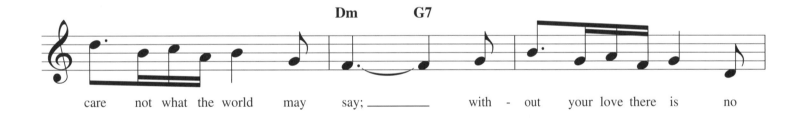

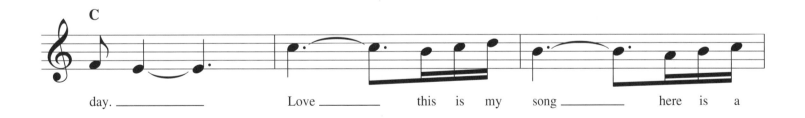

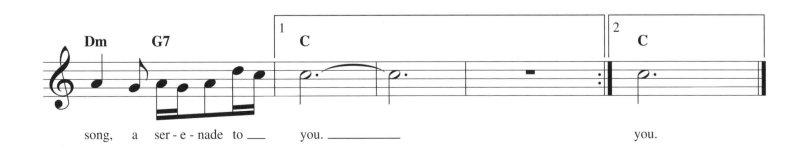

# THOSE WERE THE DAYS

Words and Music by
GENE RASKIN

**Freely**

1. Once up - on a time there was a tav - ern, where we used to raise a glass or
2. Then the bu - sy years went rush - ing by us, we lost our star - ry no - tions on the
3.,4. *(See additional lyrics)*

two. Re - mem - ber how we laughed a - way the ho - urs, and
way. If by chance I'd see you in the tav - ern, we'd

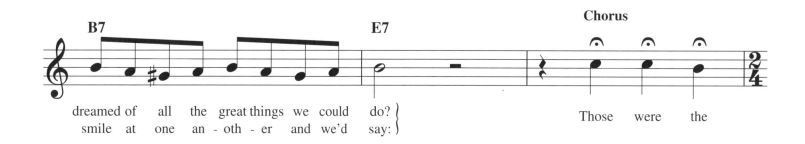

dreamed of all the great things we could do? Those were the
smile at one an - oth - er and we'd say:

**Chorus**

**Two-Beat**

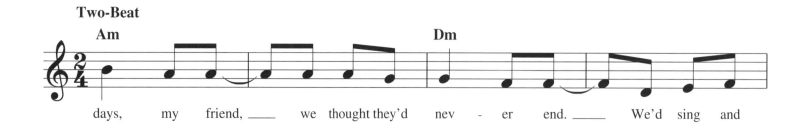

days, my friend, ___ we thought they'd nev - er end. ___ We'd sing and

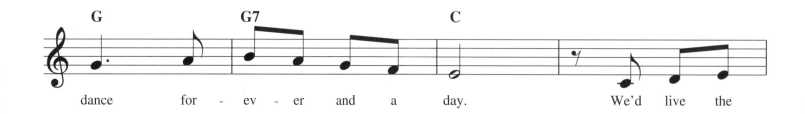

dance for - ev - er and a day. We'd live the

life we choose, __ we'd fight and nev - er lose. ____ For we are

young and sure ____ to have our way. La la la la la la __

__ la la la la la la, _____ Those were the days, oh

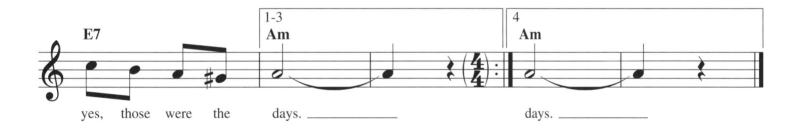

yes, those were the days. _____ days. _____

*Additional Lyrics*

3. Just tonight I stood before the tavern,
   Nothing seemed the way it used to be.
   In the glass I saw a strange reflection.
   Was that lonely fellow really me?
   *(Chorus)*

4. Through the door there came familiar laughter,
   I saw your face and heard you call my name.
   Oh, my friend, we're older but no wiser,
   For in our hearts the dreams are still the same.
   *(Chorus)*

# TIJUANA TAXI

Words by JOHNNY FLAMINGO
Music by ERVAN "BUD" COLEMAN

**Moderately**

Down in old Ti - jua - na town _____ there's this
not im - pressed, you say, _____ with a

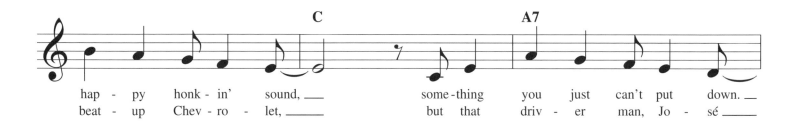

hap - py honk - in' sound, _____ some - thing you just can't put down. _____
beat - up Chev - ro - let, _____ but that driv - er man, Jo - sé _____

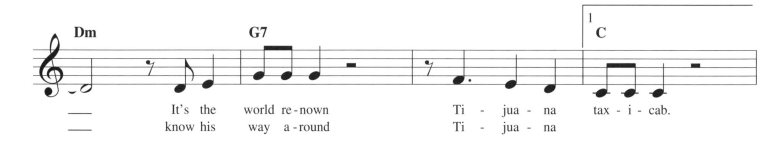

It's the world re - nown Ti - jua - na tax - i - cab.
know his way a - round Ti - jua - na

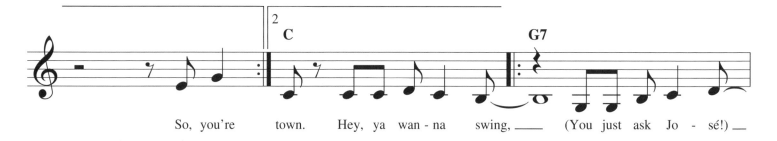

So, you're town. Hey, ya wan - na swing, _____ (You just ask Jo - sé!) _____

_____ have your - self a fling, _____ (What - cha wan - na play?) _____ meet some pret - ty thing? _____

_____ (An - y - time you say) _____ liv - in' like a king! _____ (long as you can pay.) _____

F       Fm

Pic - ture post - cards 'n' hot te - qui - la,

C    A7    Dm

French per - fume, __ man, from Ven - e - zuel - a, when you're on __ a

G7    C

Ti - jua - na tax - i ride!

{ Give those bulls a great big hand, __
{ So ya swing and go for broke, __

G7      C  A7

__ love that mar - i - ach - i band, __ but the best thing in the land __
__ not a pen - ny in your poke, __ got no cig - ar - ettes to smoke, __

Dm   1 G7      C

__ is that hand- me-down Ti - jua - na tax - i-cab.
__ but ya

2 G7

Hey, ya wan - na swing, __ had your fling, the pret - ty thing and

C

ev - 'ry-thing is ring - a - ding. O - lé!

# TRAVELIN' MAN

Words and Music by
JERRY FULLER

**Moderate Rock**

I'm a  trav - el - in'  man,  and  I've  made  a  lot  o'  stops

all  o - ver  the  world. ___  And  in  ev - er - y  port _____  I ___

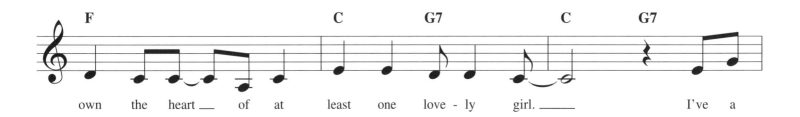

own  the  heart ___  of  at  least  one  love - ly  girl. _____  I've  a

pret - ty  se - ño - ri - ta  wait - in'  for  me ___  .  down  in  old  Mex - i - co. _

___  And  if  you're  ev - er  in  A - las - ka,  stop  and  see _____  my

cute  lit - tle  Es - ki - mo. ___  Oh,  my  sweet  frau - lein ___  down  in

Em                          F                                 3         C

Ber - lin town ___ makes my heart start to yearn. _____ And my

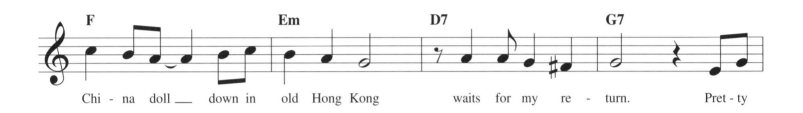

F                           Em                D7                 G7

Chi - na doll ___ down in old Hong Kong waits for my re - turn. Pret - ty

C                           Am                         C

Pol - y - ne - sian ba - by o - ver the sea, ___ I re - mem - ber the night ___

Am                           C              C7                 F

___ when we walked on the sands of Wai - ki - ki ___ and I

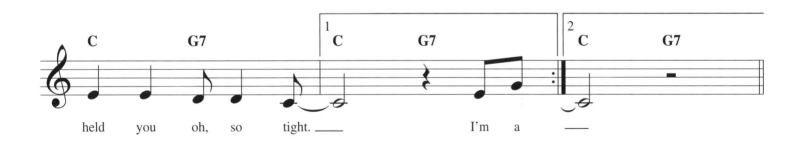

C                G7               1 C        G7         2 C        G7

held you oh, so tight. ___ I'm a ___

C                           Am                         C

{ Oh, ___ }
{ Yes, ___ } I'm a trav - el - in' man. ___

# TURN! TURN! TURN!
## (To Everything There Is a Season)

Words from the Book of Ecclesiastes
Adaptation and Music by PETE SEEGER

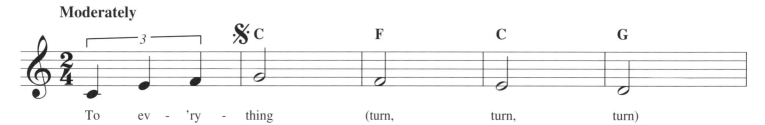

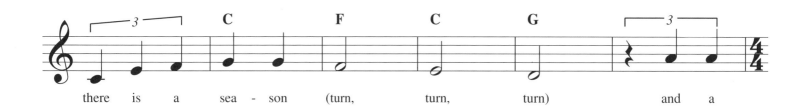

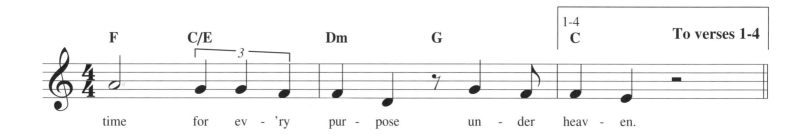

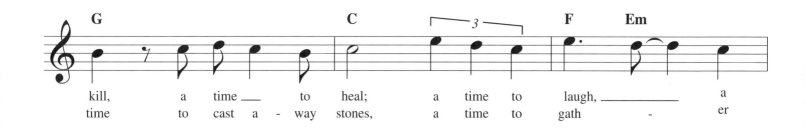

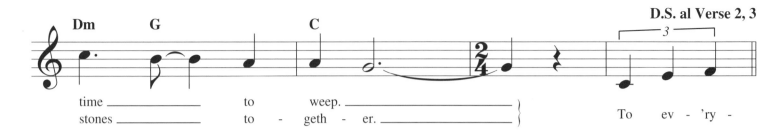

time _____ to weep. _____
stones _____ to - geth - er. _____ To ev - 'ry -

**Verse 3, 4**

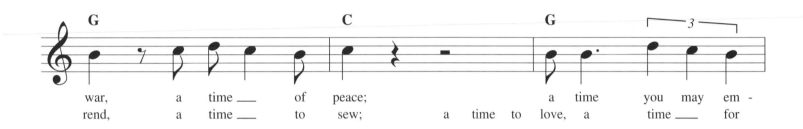

A time of love, a time ___ of hate; a time of
A time to gain, a time ___ to lose, a time to

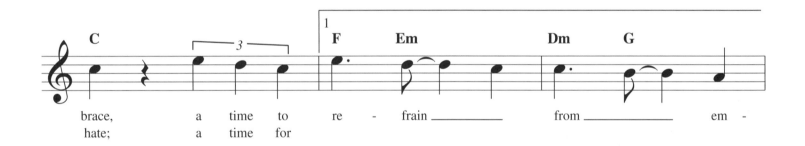

war, a time ___ of peace; a time you may em -
rend, a time ___ to sew; a time to love, a time ___ for

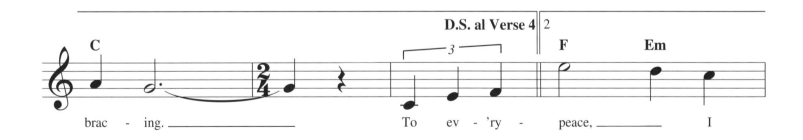

brace, a time to re - frain _____ from _____ em -
hate; a time for

**D.S. al Verse 4**

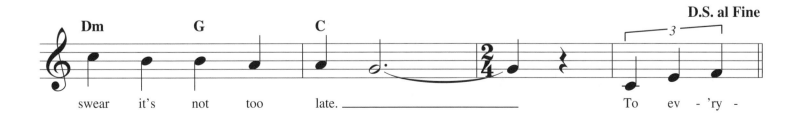

brac - ing. _____ To ev - 'ry - peace, _____ I

**D.S. al Fine**

swear it's not too late. _____ To ev - 'ry -

# THE TWIST

Words and Music by
HANK BALLARD

**Rock 'n' Roll Shuffle**

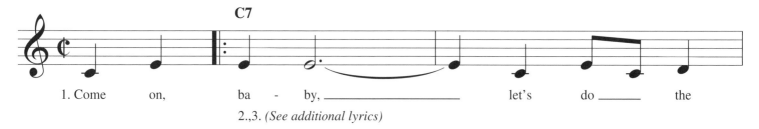

1. Come on, ba - by, _____ let's do _____ the
2.,3. *(See additional lyrics)*

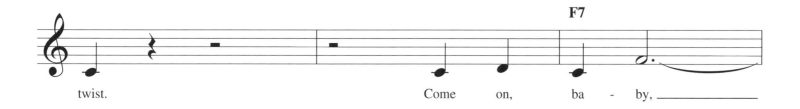

twist. Come on, ba - by, _____

___ let's do the twist. Take me by my lit - tle

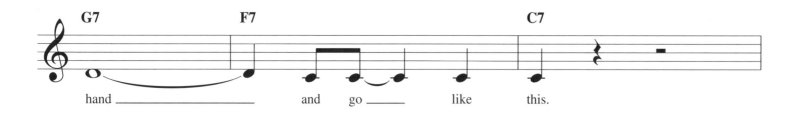

hand _____ and go _____ like this.

**Chorus**

Ee oh, twist, ba - by, ba - by,

twist. ('Round and a - round and a - round and a -) Just, _____

_____ just like this. ('Round and a - round) Come on, ____ lit - tle

miss, and do ____ the twist. ('Round and a -

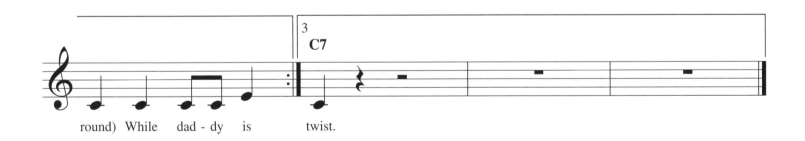

round) While dad - dy is twist.

*Additional Lyrics*

2. While daddy is sleeping and mama ain't around.
   While daddy is sleeping and mama ain't around.
   We're gonna twisty, twisty, twisty until we tear the house down.
   *Chorus*

3. You should see my little sis.
   You should see my little sis.
   She knows how to rock and she knows how to twist.
   *Chorus*

# UNCHAINED MELODY
### from the Motion Picture UNCHAINED

Lyric by HY ZARET
Music by ALEX NORTH

Flowing

Oh, my love, my dar - ling, I've hun - gered for your

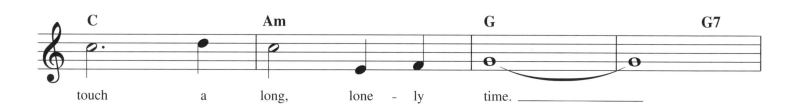

touch a long, lone - ly time. _____

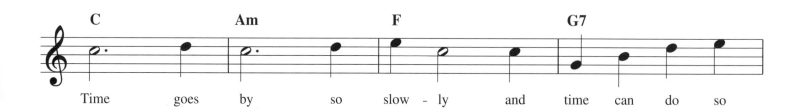

Time goes by so slow - ly and time can do so

much, are you still mine? _____ I

need your love, _____ I need your love, _____ God

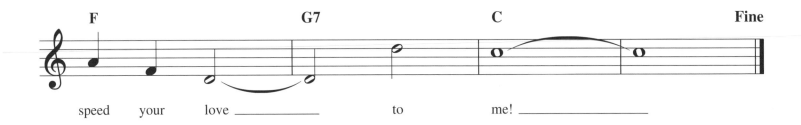

speed your love _____ to me! _____

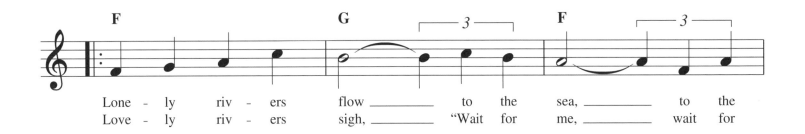

Lone - ly riv - ers flow _____ to the sea, _____ to the
Love - ly riv - ers sigh, _____ "Wait for me, _____ wait for

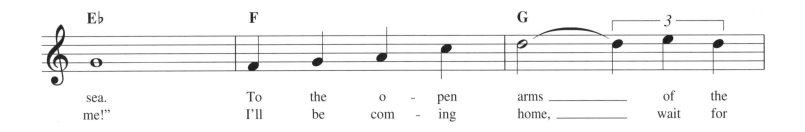

sea. To the o - pen arms _____ of the
me!" I'll be com - ing home, _____ wait for

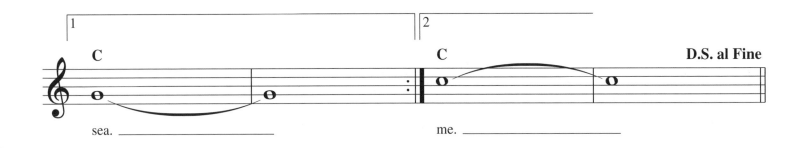

sea. _____
me. _____

# WALKIN' THE DOG

Words and Music by
RUFUS THOMAS

**Moderate Rock**

Mar - y Mack,     dressed __ in black,     sil - ver but - tons up and
Asked her mom - ma for   fif - teen     cents   to see an el - e - phant __

down her back.     How'd I know? __     Yes, she told.
jump the fence.     It jumped so high,   touched the sky,

She broke a nee - dle; now   she can't sew. __  } Walk - in' the dog. __
did - n't come     back   till the Fourth of Jul - ly. __

I'm just a - walk - in' your   dog. __                Well, if you

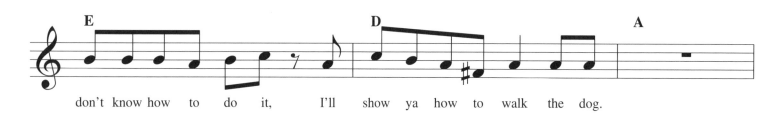

don't know how to do it,   I'll show ya how to walk the dog.

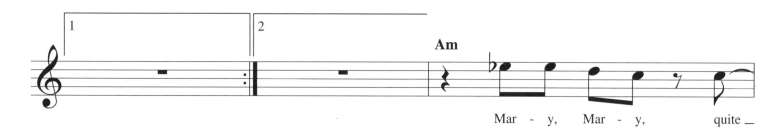

Mar - y, Mar - y,   quite __

__ con - trar - y,     how does your gar - den grow? __ (Ver - y well.)

# WHERE DID OUR LOVE GO

Words and Music by BRIAN HOLLAND,
LAMONT DOZIER and EDWARD HOLLAND

# WHITE RABBIT

Words and Music by
GRACE SLICK

**Moderately**

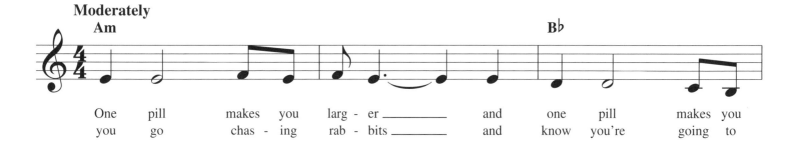

One  pill   makes  you  larg - er _____  and  one  pill    makes  you
you  go   chas - ing  rab - bits _____  and  know  you're  going  to

small.   And  the  ones  that  moth - er  gives  you   don't
fall.   Tell 'em  all  who  got  a  smok - in'  cat - er - pil - lar  has

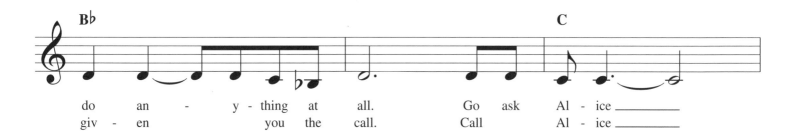

do  an - y - thing  at  all.   Go  ask  Al - ice _____
giv - en   you  the  call.   Call  Al - ice _____

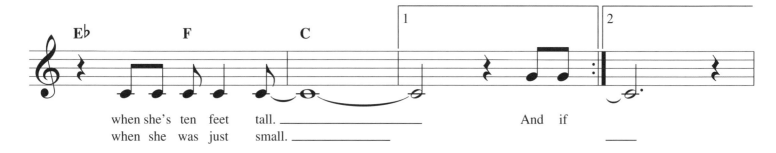

when she's  ten  feet   tall. _____       And  if
when she  was  just   small. _____

When  men  on  the  chess - board _____  get  up  and  tell  you  where  to  go. __

__  And  you've  just  had  some __  kind  of  mush - room, _____  and  your

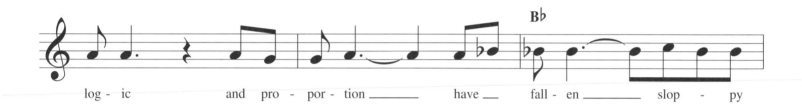

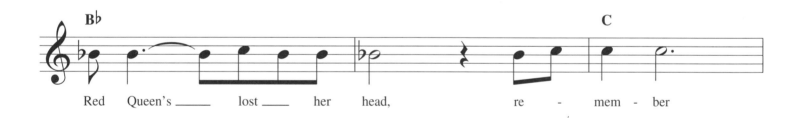

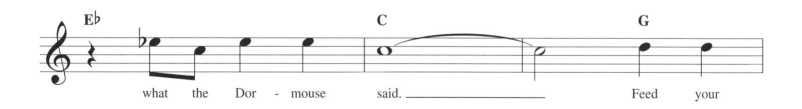

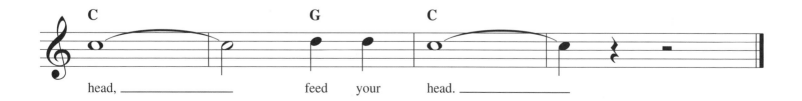

# WHO PUT THE BOMP (IN THE BOMP BA BOMP BA BOMP)

Words and Music by BARRY MANN
and GERRY GOFFIN

**Slowly**

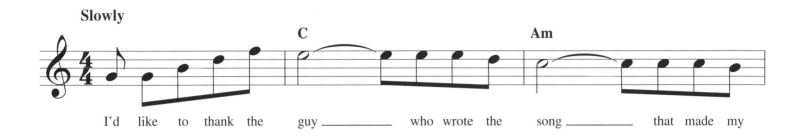

I'd like to thank the guy _____ who wrote the song _____ that made my

ba - by fall in love with me. *(Instrumental)* **With a beat**

Who put the bomp in the bomp ba bomp __ ba bomp?

Who put the ram in the ram - a - lam - a - ding - dong? Who put the bop in the

bop sh - bop __ sh - bop? Who put the dit in the dit, dit, dit, ___ dit - da?

Who was that man? I'd like to shake his hand. _____ He

made my ba - by fall in love with me. _____

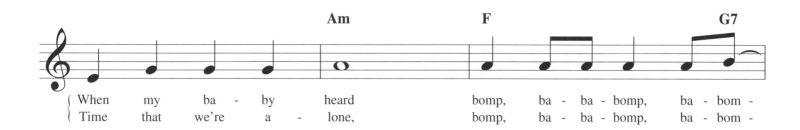

When my ba - by heard        bomp, ba - ba - bomp, ba - bom -
Time that we're a - lone,      bomp, ba - ba - bomp, ba - bom -

- ba - bomp - bomp,    ev - 'ry word went right in - to her heart. _____
- ba - bomp - bomp,    sets my ba - by's heart all a - glow. _____

____   And when she heard them sing - ing    ram - a - lam - a - lam -
____   And ev - 'ry time we dance to    ram - a - lam - a - lam -

- a - lam - a - ding - dong,    she said we'd nev - er have to
- a - lam - a - ding - dong,    she al - ways says she loves me

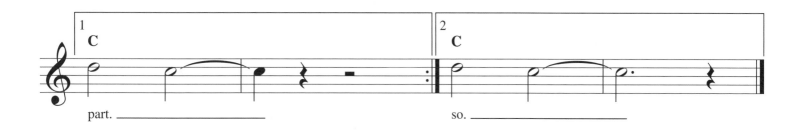

part. _____                    so. _____

# WICHITA LINEMAN

Words and Music by
JIMMY WEBB

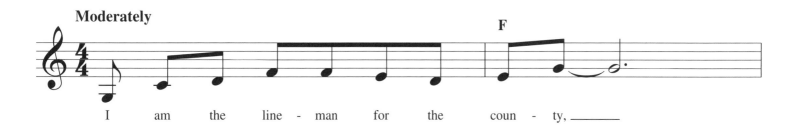

I am the line - man for the coun - ty, _____

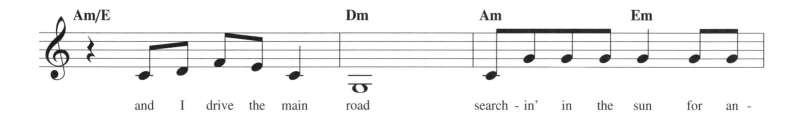

and I drive the main road    search - in' in the sun for an -

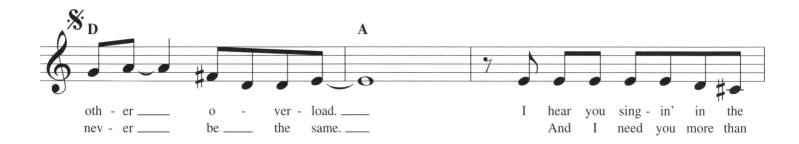

oth - er _____ o - ver - load. _____         I hear you sing - in' in the
nev - er _____ be _____ the same. _____       And I need you more than

wi - res          I can hear you through the whine, _____
want you,         and I want you for all time, _____

and the Wi - chi - ta  Line - man    is still on the line. _____
and the Wi - chi - ta  Line - man    is still on the line. _____

I know I need a small va - ca - tion, but it don't look like

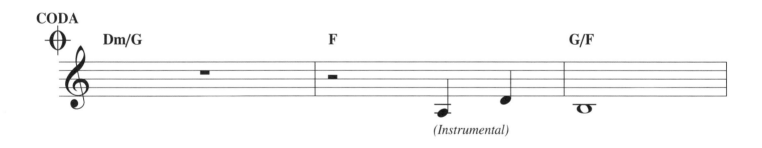

rain, and if it snows, that stretch down south will

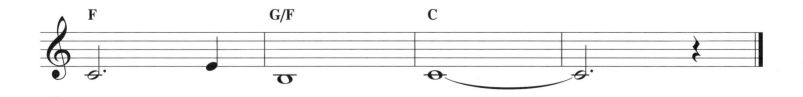

*(Instrumental)*

# WORDS OF LOVE

Words and Music by
JOHN PHILLIPS

**Moderate Ragtime tempo**

Words of love __ so soft and ten - der won't win a girl's heart __ an - y - more. __

__ If you love __ her, then you __ must send __ her

some - where where she's __ nev - er been be - fore. __ Worn - out phras - es and

long - ing gaz - es won't get you where you ought to go. __ *No!*

Words of love __ soft and ten - der, won't __ win her. __

**With a Rock feel**

__ You ought to know by now. __

You ought to know. __ You ought to know by now. __ Words of love __

soft and ten - der, won't __ win her __ an - y -

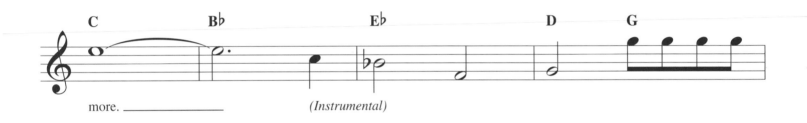

more. _____ (Instrumental)

You ___ ought to know by _____ now. _____

___ You ought to know. __ You ___ ought to know by now. __ Words of love __

soft and ten - der won't win a girl's heart ___ an - y - more. ___

If you love ___ her, then you ___ must send ___ her some-where where she's nev - er

been be - fore. ___ Worn-out phras - es and long - ing gaz - es won't

get you where you ought to go. ___ Words of love ___

soft and ten - der won't ___ win her ___ an - y -

more. An - y - more. ___

# YESTERDAY

Words and Music by JOHN LENNON
and PAUL McCARTNEY

# WOULDN'T IT BE NICE

Words and Music by BRIAN WILSON,
TONY ASHER and MIKE LOVE

**Moderate Shuffle**

Would - n't it be nice if we were old - er, then ___ we would - n't
nice if we could wake ___ up in ___ the morn - ing

have to wait ___ so long. _____ And would - n't it be nice to live to - geth -
when the day ___ is new. _____ And af - ter that to spend the day to - geth -

- er in ___ the kind of world where we'd ___ be - long. _____
- er, hold ___ each oth - er close the whole ___ night through. ___

Though it's gon - na make it that much bet - ter when we can say good - night and
The hap - py times to - geth - er we'd been spend - ing, I wish that ev - 'ry kiss was

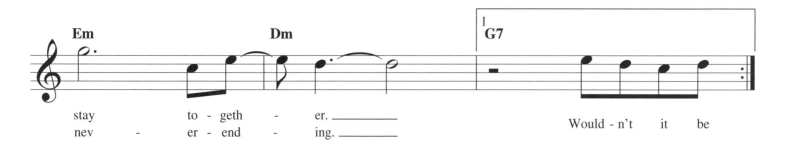

stay to - geth - er. _____
nev - er end - ing. _____

Would - n't it be

Oh would - n't it ___ be ___ nice? _____

203

# You've Made Me So Very Happy

Words and Music by BERRY GORDY, FRANK E. WILSON,
BRENDA HOLLOWAY and PATRICE HOLLOWAY

**Moderately**

I lost at love ____ be-fore, got mad and

closed ____ the door, _____ but you said try just once more.

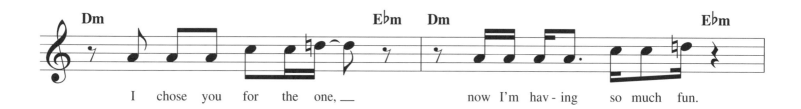

I chose you for the one, ____ now I'm hav-ing so much fun.

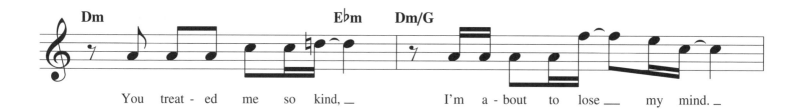

You treat-ed me so kind, ____ I'm a-bout to lose ____ my mind. ____

You made me ____ so ____ ver-y hap-py. I'm so glad you ____

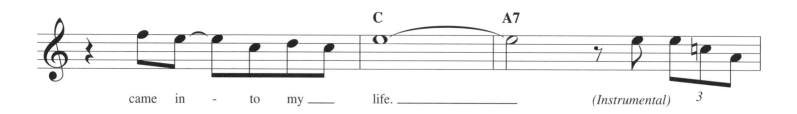

came in-to my ____ life. _____ (Instrumental)

The oth-ers were un-true, but when it

205

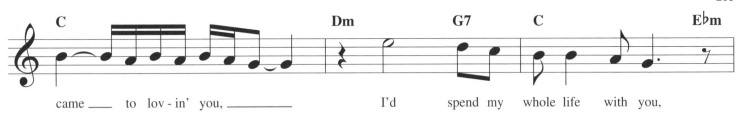

came ___ to lov-in' you, _____ I'd spend my whole life with you,

'cause you came and you took con-trol. ___ You touched my ver-y soul. ___

You al-ways showed me that ___ lov-ing you is where it's at. You made me ___ so ___

ver-y hap-py. I'm so glad you ___ came in-to my ___

life. *(Instrumental)* Thank you,

ba - by! ___ *(Instrumental)* Yeah, yeah.

*(Instrumental)* I love you so much, it seems ___ *(Instrumental)* you're e-ven in my dreams. ___ I can

hear, _____ ba - by, I ____ can hear you're call - ing me. *(Instrumental)*

I'm so in love with you. _____ All I ev - er want to do __ is

thank you ba - by, thank you, ba - by! *(Instrumental)*

You made me __ so __

ver - y hap - py. I'm so glad you came in - to my

life. *(Instrumental)* You made me ___ so ___

ver - y ____ hap - py.     You made __ me so,     so ver - y hap - py, ba - by.

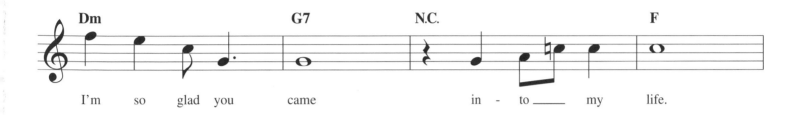

I'm  so  glad you  came                in - to ____ my  life.

Mmm, _____ I wan - na  thank you, girl!

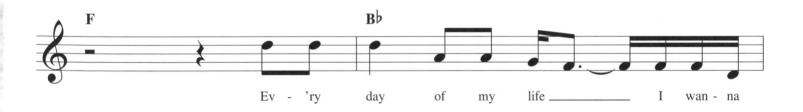

Ev - 'ry  day  of  my  life _____ I  wan - na

thank  you. ___     You made me  so _____ ver - y hap - py.

Oh,  I  wan - na spend  my  life ____  thank - ing  you. _____ Thank  you,

**Repeat and Fade**

ba - by! _____  Thank  you,  ba - by! _____ Thank  you,

# CHORD SPELLER

### C chords

| | |
|---|---|
| C | C–E–G |
| Cm | C–E♭–G |
| C7 | C–E–G–B♭ |
| Cdim | C–E♭–G♭ |
| C+ | C–E–G# |

### C# or D♭ chords

| | |
|---|---|
| C# | C#–F–G# |
| C#m | C#–E–G# |
| C#7 | C#–F–G#–B |
| C#dim | C#–E–G |
| C#+ | C#–F–A |

### D chords

| | |
|---|---|
| D | D–F#–A |
| Dm | D–F–A |
| D7 | D–F#–A–C |
| Ddim | D–F–A♭ |
| D+ | D–F#–A# |

### E♭ chords

| | |
|---|---|
| E♭ | E♭–G–B♭ |
| E♭m | E♭–G♭–B♭ |
| E♭7 | E♭–G–B♭–D♭ |
| E♭dim | E♭–G♭–A |
| E♭+ | E♭–G–B |

### E chords

| | |
|---|---|
| E | E–G#–B |
| Em | E–G–B |
| E7 | E–G#–B–D |
| Edim | E–G–B♭ |
| E+ | E–G#–C |

### F chords

| | |
|---|---|
| F | F–A–C |
| Fm | F–A♭–C |
| F7 | F–A–C–E♭ |
| Fdim | F–A♭–B |
| F+ | F–A–C# |

### F# or G♭ chords

| | |
|---|---|
| F# | F#–A#–C# |
| F#m | F#–A–C# |
| F#7 | F#–A#–C#–E |
| F#dim | F#–A–C |
| F#+ | F#–A#–D |

### G chords

| | |
|---|---|
| G | G–B–D |
| Gm | G–B♭–D |
| G7 | G–B–D–F |
| Gdim | G–B♭–D♭ |
| G+ | G–B–D# |

### G# or A♭ chords

| | |
|---|---|
| A♭ | A♭–C–E♭ |
| A♭m | A♭–B–E♭ |
| A♭7 | A♭–C–E♭–G♭ |
| A♭dim | A♭–B–D |
| A♭+ | A♭–C–E |

### A chords

| | |
|---|---|
| A | A–C#–E |
| Am | A–C–E |
| A7 | A–C#–E–G |
| Adim | A–C–E♭ |
| A+ | A–C#–F |

### B♭ chords

| | |
|---|---|
| B♭ | B♭–D–F |
| B♭m | B♭–D♭–F |
| B♭7 | B♭–D–F–A♭ |
| B♭dim | B♭–D♭–E |
| B♭+ | B♭–D–F# |

### B chords

| | |
|---|---|
| B | B–D#–F# |
| Bm | B–D–F# |
| B7 | B–D#–F#–A |
| Bdim | B–D–F |
| B+ | B–D#–G |

Important Note: A slash chord (C/E, G/B) tells you that a certain bass note is to be played under a particular harmony. In the case of C/E, the chord is C and the bass note is E.